Joy by a Roaring Campfire

Devotions for Campers

Nancy Bell Kimsey

Published by Pine Warbler Publications
Fuquay-Varina, North Carolina, United States of
America

First Printing, 2021

Cover Art by Savannah Battle
Cover Design by Nathan Stikeleather

ISBN #9781736773123 (eBook)
ISBN #9781736773130 (Paperback)

To Samuel and Ethan:
May your lives be filled with joy as you explore
God's wonderful creation.

Only Passing Through

By faith Abraham, when called to go to a place he would later receive as his inheritance, obeyed and went, even though he did not know where he was going. By faith he made his home in the promised land like a stranger in a foreign country; he lived in tents, as did Isaac and Jacob, who were heirs with him of the same promise...admitting that they were foreigners and strangers on earth. Hebrews 11:8-9, 13

What is the greatest number of days in a row that you have ever slept in a tent? Did you change campsites every day? If so, you likely packed as few items as possible in order to break camp quickly and travel light. Abraham spent most of his life living in tents, although the land through which he traveled was the land that God had clearly promised to his family. The eleventh chapter of the Book of Hebrews includes Abraham, his son Isaac, and his grandson Jacob in a list of heroes of faith. These individuals are commended, not only because they demonstrated their faith through obedience, but also because they considered themselves to be foreigners and strangers on earth. They were only passing through.

To "travel light" through life, spiritually speaking, is more than embracing minimalism and paring down the total amount of our possessions. Light living cultivates the idea that we are stewards, rather than owners, of everything that we have. We take care of our belongings and don't use them wastefully, but we also are willing to give them up if God leads us to share. "If anyone has material possessions and sees a brother or sister

1

in need but has no pity on them, how can the love of God be in that person?" (1 John 3:17) We also don't insist on grabbing the best seats or the largest cookie! "Then he said to them, 'Watch out!' Be on your guard against all kinds of greed; life does not consist in an abundance of possessions.'" (Luke 12:15)

After Abraham became wealthy, he owned so many animals that the land could not support both himself and his nephew Lot. When they decided to go their separate ways, Abraham allowed Lot to choose his portion of land first. Lot chose the fertile plain of the Jordan , seemingly a better choice, but Lot had deliberately chosen to pitch his tents near the evil and corrupt city of Sodom. God reminded Abraham that He would continue to bless him. "All the land that you see I will give to you and your offspring forever. I will make your offspring like the dust of the earth, so that if anyone could count the dust, then your offspring could be counted." (Genesis 13:15-16) In the very next chapter of Genesis, we learn that Lot and his family and goods were seized and carried off during a battle, and eventually Sodom was utterly destroyed.

Meditating upon the brevity of life, the joys of eternity with Christ, and the unending faithfulness of God will enable us to view this world as our temporary dwelling and our possessions as a gift on loan from the Lord.

Prayer for Today:

Dear God, help me to travel light as I walk
through this world. Thank you that You
promise to provide for all of my needs. May I
never try to hold on selfishly to that which will
not last forever. Amen.

2

Contentment

But godliness with contentment is great gain. For we brought nothing into the world, and we can take nothing out of it. But if we have food and clothing, we will be content with that. Those who want to get rich fall into temptation and a trap and into many foolish and harmful desires that plunge people into ruin and destruction. 1Timothy 6:6-9

Are you a beach person or a mountain person? The beach person will treasure any opportunity to soak up the sun at the ocean's edge or jump through the surf, while the mountain person gains satisfaction from hiking to an overlook or resting by a stream. Camping in either location can bring happiness, peace, and contentment. Although it may cost some money to drive to your desired location, the beauty of the natural setting is a free gift from God.

The apostle Paul reminded Timothy that "godliness with contentment is great gain." (1 Timothy 6:6) Notice the word *with* in the verse. If we are content but not godly, then we have made the mistake of becoming satisfied with a life that does not honor God. If we are godly but not content, we may have jumped through some religious behavioral hoops without ever achieving a restful spirit. Paul provides Timothy (and us) with important insight about contentment. First, it's good to remember that we enter and leave this world with nothing.

"For we brought nothing into this world, and we can take nothing out of it." (1 Timothy 6:7) Second, basic necessities such as food and clothing are all that we truly need. "But if we have food and clothing, we will be content with that." (1 Timothy6:8) Third, the desire for riches can stir up many other "foolish and harmful desires that plunge people into ruin and destruction." (1 Timothy 6:9)

Are you smelling sea air and tasting salt water today? Thank the Lord for these wonderful experiences and praise Him for his creation. Push back against the temptation to crave a fancier beach house or a new convertible to zip around in. Are you enjoying the spray from a waterfall and the beauty of autumn leaves today? Remind yourself that even campers with the most expensive gear will observe the same view as you. If you are able to achieve both godliness and contentment, there will truly be great gain. "Keep your lives free from the love of money and be content with what you have, for God has said, 'Never will I leave you; never will I forsake you.'" (Hebrews 13:5)

Prayer for Today:

Dear God, I have far to go in achieving godliness. May I become more like You as I carefully read your Word and apply it to my life. I also have far to go in achieving contentment. Make me aware of times that I am dissatisfied or have developed a love of money. You have freely given so much to me. Help me to be grateful and content. Amen.

Smoke Follows Beauty

Because of your great compassion you did not abandon them in the wilderness. By day the pillar of cloud did not fail to guide them on their path, nor the pillar of fire by night to shine on the way they were to take. Nehemiah 9:19

"Smoke follows beauty." That's a pretty ridiculous statement, yet it is often proclaimed jokingly around a campfire. We all know that smoke from a fire will generally travel upward unless a breeze pushes the smoke in a different direction, and most of us aren't at our most beautiful while on a campout. So if the smoke could indeed seek out beauty, it might choose to just ignore everyone sitting around the fire and focus solely on rising heavenward to the glorious panoply of stars.

When the people of Israel wandered in the desert, they were led by a vertical pillar of cloud by day and a pillar of fire at night, both ascending to the skies. The sovereign God used these visible manifestations of his presence to remind them of his nearness and to direct the people as to when to move forward. Nehemiah looked back at that time in history as proof of the Lord's great compassion. "Because of your great compassion you did not abandon them in the wilderness. By day the pillar of cloud did not fail to guide them on their path, nor the pillar of fire by night to shine on the way they were to take." (Nehemiah 9:19)

It has been well said that God wants us to know his will for our lives even more than we do! He may not make the path obvious each day, but He is not a cruel or frustrating Father. James 1:5 promises, "If any of you lacks wisdom, you should ask God, who gives generously to all without finding fault, and it will be given to you." Wisdom can be gleaned from the study of Scripture and times of prayer, from the advice of wise counselors, and from the opening and closing of doors of opportunity as we step forward one day at a time.

Prayer for Today:

Dear God, you are the Lord over all that you
have created. You were able to supernaturally
lead the people of Israel using columns of
cloud and fire, and You faithfully directed them
through the desert. I believe that You care for
me just as much as You cared for the Israelites,
so I trust You to send guidance for my
pathways and assurance that You are with me.
Please help me to faithfully step forward as
You lead. Amen.

Go to the Source

Above all, you must understand that no prophecy of Scripture came about by the prophet's own interpretation of things. For prophecy never had its origin in the human will, but prophets, though human, spoke from God as they were carried along by the Holy Spirit.
2 Peter 1:20-21

On camping vacations, we sometimes have the opportunity to visit museums and historical sites along the way. Many of these places use quotations from primary sources in their displays. For example, at the Gettysburg Battlefield National Historic Site, instead of merely displaying information concerning the mindset of soldiers far from home, large quotations from the letters that actual soldiers sent to their loved ones are etched on the walls. The Ellis Island Museum of Immigration takes this a step further and includes recordings of primary source material performed by actors. All this makes the exhibits far more interesting and accurate. Going directly to the source leaves less room for false interpretations of historical events.

If we want to accurately follow God's plan for humanity, we must go to God's designated source of information: the Bible. While sermons, religious podcasts, and our friends' advice can all be helpful, it's crucial to read the Scriptures for yourself and ask the Holy Spirit to enlighten you as you read. You will find that the Scriptures have remarkable continuity, even though they were written by at least 35 authors over a period of about 1500 years. Very specific details concerning the life and death of Jesus were prophesied hundreds of years before his birth, and the attributes of God (such as his holiness, faithfulness, and love) are evident throughout the Old and New Testaments.

Jesus promised the Jews who believed in him, "If you hold to my teaching, you are really my disciples. Then you will know the truth, and the truth will set you free." (John 8:31-32) Knowing the truth, living in freedom - what a privilege to know that these are actually attainable as we follow Christ in discipleship and learn from him.

Prayer for Today:

Dear God, your Scriptures are a perfect guidebook . May I faithfully study them, rather than relying on the thoughts of other people or the popular ideas of our culture. Thank you that the truth will set me free if I carefully follow your Word as a devoted disciple. Amen.

Meaningful Names

And the name of the city from that time will be: THE LORD IS THERE. Ezekiel 48:35

Some national parks have names that draw you in with their beauty, such as Gates of the Arctic and Great Smoky Mountains, while others like Death Valley and Badlands sound rather foreboding. Haleakala, Denali, and Cuyahoga Valley reflect the heritage of the native people groups who first lived there, and Arches and Big Bend describe natural features found in the parks.

Have you ever been reading through a section of the Bible that contains a list of genealogies or rituals, and you find that your mind is wandering away to side topics, such as what to cook for dinner? Then suddenly, a verse jumps off the page, filled with meaning? The final chapter of Ezekiel is primarily a detailed description of the division of land to the 12 tribes of Israel. The book ends with the allocation of names for the gates of Jerusalem (also named after the tribes) and one remarkable concluding statement: "And the name of the city from that time will be: THE LORD IS THERE." (Ezekiel 48:35) Jerusalem was established as the holy city of the Jews, its spiritual center. But the Bible is clear that the Lord is with all those who trust in Him, wherever they may live or travel.

9

God the Father, God the Son, and God the Holy Spirit are all there for those who believe by faith.

* "So do not fear, for I am with you; do not be dismayed, for I am your God. I will strengthen you and help you; I will uphold you with my righteous right hand." (Isaiah 41:10)

* "That night the Lord appeared to him and said, 'I am the God of your father Abraham. Do not be afraid, for I am with you. I will bless you and will increase the number of your descendants for the sake of my servant Abraham.'" (Genesis 26:24)

* "Therefore go and make disciples of all nations, baptizing them in the name of the Father and of the Son and of the Holy Spirit, and teaching them to obey everything I have commanded you. And surely I am with you always, to the very end of the age." (Matthew 28:19-20)

* "And I will ask the Father, and he will give you another advocate to help you and be with you forever." (John 14:16)

Prayer for Today:

Dear God, there are truths to be found in every part of your Word. Help me not to ignore entire sections of the Scriptures. Thank you that You promised to be with the city of Jerusalem in a special way, and thank you that You also dwell in the heart of every believer. I count on your presence today. Amen.

Silly Skits

A cheerful heart is good medicine, but a crushed spirit dries up the bones. Proverbs 17:22

Campfire time at Scout camp or church camp often includes having groups create silly skits or stories to perform for the others. These light and goofy performances won't ever win an Oscar, but they generate some fun memories. You've probably heard the saying, "Laughter is the best medicine." Many scientific studies have concluded that humor has many specific health benefits, such as lowering blood pressure, reducing stress, and releasing endorphins in your brain. Even centuries ago, the writer of Proverbs declared, "A cheerful heart is good medicine". (Proverbs 17:22) In today's busy world, it's not often that we hear a story or joke that is funny enough to cause us to double over with laughter. But when we are relaxing around a campfire, there is usually enough time and mental space to enjoy life and to laugh out loud with friends or family.

Humor is best when it is not at the expense of another person. Although you may insist, "I'm not laughing *at* you, I'm laughing *with* you," many stories that one person might consider to be good-natured ribbing can bring distress to others. Some tales can have a cutting undercurrent, causing the

11

subject to look foolish in the eyes of their children or peers. It's always best to stop and consider what the response will be from the subject of your joke.

The counterpart is also true: we should not take ourselves too seriously. If we are constantly trying to uphold an image of personal perfection, we will be too easily offended. Proverbs 29:23 states, "Pride brings a person low, but the lowly in spirit gain honor." It's good to relax and allow others to hear about some of our less-than-stellar moments.

Finally, true joy is deeper and more sustaining than the levity of a skit or even the temporary happiness that comes from positive circumstances. When the laughter dies down or our life situations change, joy can still remain. Jesus said, "If you keep my commands, you will remain in my love, just as I have kept my Father's commands and remain in his love. I have told you this so that my joy may be in you and that your joy may be complete. My command is this: Love each other as I have loved you." (John 15:10-12)

Prayer for Today:

Dear God, thank you that You promise joy to those who keep your commands. Help me to be obedient to your Word this day, and help me to love others as you have loved me. Amen.

Pizzaville National Park?

Be careful not to practice your righteousness in front of others to be seen by them. If you do, you will have no reward from your Father in heaven. So when you give to the needy, do not announce it with trumpets, as the hypocrites do in the synagogues and on the streets, to be honored by others. Truly I tell you, they have received their reward in full. But when you give to the needy, do not let your left hand know what your right hand is doing, so that your giving may be in secret. Then your Father, who sees what is done in secret, will reward you.
Matthew 6:1-4

Can you imagine Yellowstone National Park receiving a new name because of a multi-million dollar donation by a chain of pizza restaurants? The move might turn out to be an advertising windfall for the donor, but citizens would likely be outraged. Sports stadiums, concert amphitheaters, bowl games, and other venues and events are often renamed when advertising deals are signed with corporate sponsors. Companies who wish to sponsor a New Year's Day bowl game can expect to pay more than 25 million dollars for the privilege. For some sponsors, the advertising investment pays off with newfound name recognition and increased sales revenue. For others, the outlay of funds is a financial bust.

The Bible condemns self-promotion and outward shows of religious generosity. We are promised that "pride goes before destruction, a haughty spirit before a fall." (Proverbs 16:18)

Jesus assured his listeners that those who publicly announce their charitable gifts will only receive rewards here on Earth. We might enjoy box seat tickets to a great game or hear the adulation of a television reporter as she announces our donation. But when we give generously in secret, God sees what we have done, and He will reward us.

What types of rewards might we receive from God? In this life, we would receive inner joy and satisfaction from helping others and advancing the kingdom of God. The clandestine nature of our giving would allow us to avoid media attention. We would also never have to wonder if others truly enjoy our friendship or merely wish to hang out with someone who has financial clout. The specific nature of future heavenly rewards remains to be seen, but we can be certain that the rewards are fair and meaningful.

Today, look for ways that you can secretly give to others, and push back against the natural inclination to pat yourself on the back or call attention to your gift. As Jesus reminded his disciples in Matthew 10:8, "Freely you have received; freely give."

Prayer for Today:

Dear Lord, it is so easy to promote myself or
expect others to thank me publicly for gifts that
should be given freely and in secret. May I
only seek the eternal rewards that come from
You. Show me specific ways that I can help
others with no expectation of recognition here
on Earth. Amen.

Coming on the Clouds

Then will appear the sign of the Son of Man in heaven. And then all the peoples of the earth will mourn when they see the Son of Man coming on the clouds of heaven, with power and great glory. And he will send his angels with a loud trumpet call, and they will gather his elect from the four winds, from one end of the heavens to the other.
Matthew 24:30-31

Have you ever looked for animal shapes in fluffy cumulus clouds? One person might see the shape of a rabbit, while their friend might insist that they see a bear. But if the clouds become more dense and threatening, it's time to get up from your blanket and head to shelter.

One day, Jesus will return to Earth, "coming on the clouds of heaven, with power and great glory." (Matthew 24:30) This prophecy was spoken of by Jesus himself as He taught his disciples on the Mount of Olives. The second coming of Christ is also clearly predicted in Revelation 1:7. "'Look, he is coming with the clouds,' and 'every eye will see him, even those who pierced him.'" Jesus also predicted this event while being interrogated by Caiaphas the high priest just before the crucifixion. When Caiaphas asked Jesus to clearly state whether or not he was the Messiah, Jesus responded, "I say to all of you: From now on you will see the Son of Man sitting at the right hand of the Mighty One and coming on the clouds of heaven." (Matthew 26:64). Caiaphas does not laugh at this response but tears his clothes in anger, accusing Jesus of blasphemy. Caiaphas knew that Jesus, by calling himself the Son of Man and speaking of his future entrance on the clouds, was directly referring to Daniel's messianic prophecy in Daniel 7. "In my vision at night I looked, and there before me was one like a son of man, coming with the clouds of heaven. He approached the Ancient of Days and was led into his presence. He was given authority, glory and sovereign power; all nations and peoples of every language worshiped him." (Daniel 7:13-14)

Jesus can never be considered to be merely a good man. He directly claimed to be divine. Either He was telling the truth and deserves our worship, or He lied and is unworthy of being respected or followed. Every promise and prediction in the Scriptures have been fulfilled or will be fulfilled in the future. Truly, Jesus will return on the clouds some day in power and glory. Worship and enjoy fellowship with Him now.

Prayer for Today:

Dear God, I believe the words of Jesus that He
will return some day. Thank you that I can
depend on this future reality. Thank you also
that I don't have to fear Christ's return because
my sins have been forgiven through faith in
Him.   Amen.

The Golden Hour

Teach us to number our days, that we may gain a heart of wisdom.
Psalm 90:12

Photographers call the twilight period "The Golden Hour" because natural light is warm and flattering when the sun is close to the horizon. It's the perfect time to snap a few family photos in a meadow or take your dog for a stroll or sit by an overlook. There are technically three measures of twilight: civil twilight (the moment when the sun has dipped less than 6 degrees below the horizon), nautical twilight (between 6 and 12 degrees), and astronomical twilight (12-18 degrees). Some weather websites will actually tell you, day by day, exactly how many minutes and seconds shorter or longer the next day will be (depending on the season.)

But what if humans could receive messages that would foretell the exact number of years or days remaining in our lives? I wouldn't want to know this information. However, I do need to constantly be reminded of the brevity of life, in order to not waste entire hours or days scrolling through social media, lounging in front of the television, or stewing over a frustrating situation. Those who face life-threatening illnesses often shuffle their activities and priorities in order to make room for that which suddenly seems to be most important.

17

There are at least three areas of life that I often neglect, citing lack of time, that could easily be enlarged and enriched if I would eliminate other activities that clutter up my time and mental energy. First, prayer time: getting away for more than just a moment or two to seriously pray for individuals and our world, and also to simply be still and listen. Second, reconciliation: forgiving others and ourselves, deliberately reaching out to restore broken relationships. Third, service: participating in everything from small acts of kindness to responsibilities that involve planning and commitment.

Jesus said, "As long as it is day, we must do the works of him who sent me. Night is coming, when no one can work." (John 9:4) Now is the Golden Hour.

Prayer for Today:

Dear God, each hour is a gift from you, and I know that You have provided enough time to do everything that is a part of your will for my life. Help me not to make excuses or fill my hours with the fluff of life. Amen.

I Wish You Could See This

However, I consider my life worth nothing to me; my only aim is to finish the race and complete the task the Lord Jesus has given me-the task of testifying to the good news of God's grace. Acts 20:24

When I stand at a scenic overlook, gazing at a breathtaking vista, my first reaction is to think, "God's creation is amazing!" My second reaction is to grab my cell phone and take some photos. Soon afterward, I send the photos to my family members or post on social media, with the underlying message being "I wish you could see this!" Or if I find an amazing bargain at a local store, I want to spread the news far and wide. So why is it that I am far less interested or even unwilling to share the best news of all - the good news that new life and forgiveness of sins are available through faith in Jesus?

Somehow I have been led to believe that religion (like politics) is an inappropriate topic of discussion. I act as if most people are satisfied with their inner lives and do not really want to hear what I might have to say. Yet when I listen to the conversations of others and look into their eyes, I can sense a need to personally connect to the God who created them and loves them. While I should never come across as "holier than thou" or proclaim my message in an annoying way, telling others about the opportunity to find peace with God and purpose in life should be something that I am willing, even excited to do. This is truly good news, far greater than news of a store bargain or a beautiful vacation destination.

In many cases, we must earn the right to share our good news with someone by being their friend, interacting in a gracious and kind manner, and living a life that honors God. In other situations, we may feel an inner prompting to share with someone who is a complete stranger. Often if we will just ask someone the simple question, "Is there anything that I can pray about for you?" the person will gratefully accept our offer. At that point, we must be careful to truly listen to their needs, pray with them briefly on the spot, and then remember to pray for them in the future, whether or not they are open to future conversations.

On the first Christmas, the angel told the shepherds, *Do not be afraid. I bring you good news that will cause great joy for all the people. Today in the town of David a Savior has been born to you; he is the Messiah, the Lord.* (Luke 2:10-11) Tell the good news. The world needs joy!

Prayer for Today:

Dear Jesus, your birth was good news for the
shepherds and for us, because You truly were
the Messiah who would make a way for
mankind to find peace with You. You have
taken the burden of our sins upon yourself, and
when we believe in You we find new life and
life eternal. Help me to be aware of those who
are seeking You, and give me love, grace, and
boldness to share the good news. Amen.

Step Out into Something New

You will go out in joy and be led forth in peace; the mountains and hills will burst into song before you, and all the trees of the field will clap their hands. Isaiah 55:12

At the beginning of my junior year of high school, a local Explorer Scout group that had previously been all male made the decision to go co-ed. My friend Diane and I had both been Girl Scouts for many years, but the idea of camping with boys (and a chaperone, of course) sounded like a lot more fun. We were also excited that this troop specialized in backpacking. No more time wasted selling cookies or earning merit badges - nothing but backpacking at least once a month in the fall and spring. So we gathered up our courage and went to the inaugural meeting, only to discover that we were the only two girls there!

Eventually a few more girls joined, and soon the weekend of our first backpacking trip arrived. I had not packed enough clothing layers, and as we sat around the campfire, one of the guys loaned me his extra jacket. The slight bit of awkwardness among the group that first evening was broken by laughter when another boy suddenly blurted out, "Hey, Brian, how come you never loaned *me* your jacket?"

New situations can feel uncomfortable, and not everyone is an extrovert. But when we feel an inner nudging to step out and introduce ourself, join a Bible Study group, volunteer, or speak up for someone who is being bullied, it's important to follow through. If God has put the idea in your heart and mind, then listening to that inner tug can lead to joy, grace, and fulfillment for you and for others.

"And pray for us, too, that God may open a door for our message." (Colossians 4:3)

Prayer for Today:

Dear God, there are times when I can feel an urge to do something unexpected. Help me to know when this urge has come from You, and help me to have the boldness to step forward in obedience and walk through the open door that You have provided. I trust You to enable me to accomplish all that You have called me to do. Amen.

Safety Net

Two are better than one, because they have a good return for their labor: If either of them falls down, one can help the other up. But pity anyone who falls and has no one to help them up. Ecclesiastes 4:9-10

Airline pilots are required to file a flight plan before takeoff for several reasons: avoiding air congestion, insuring smooth transitions between pairs of air traffic controllers along the route, and as a record in case the plane never arrives at its intended destination. Hikers who travel in remote areas are also encouraged to tell someone of their planned route and expected time or day of return as a similar kind of safety net. Yet every year there are news repots of hikers who lose their lives because they are injured or lost, and no one finds them until it is too late.

There are a number of ways to create a safety net for our spiritual lives in order to avoid falling into destructive habits, doctrinal error, or just plain laziness. One option is to meet with another individual on a regular basis, with the intent of sharing goals in our faith journey and helping each other follow through on those goals. We can join a small group or Bible study. I know a group of young mothers who meet virtually every Wednesday night and are able to connect with friends who have moved to other states and study the Bible while the kids are in bed. Be creative, think outside the box, but find a way to create some accountability for yourself.

Remember, an accountability partner is not supposed to discourage or deride if their associate doesn't completely reach certain goals. But it's important that this person feels able and willing to be gently honest. The Bible is our source of truth, and using God's Word as our guide in any accountability relationship is crucial.

As Paul wrote to the Ephesian believers, "Then we will no longer be infants, tossed back and forth by the waves, and blown here and there by every wind of teaching and by the cunning and craftiness of people in their deceitful scheming. Instead, speaking the truth in love, we will grow to become in every respect the mature body of him who is the head, that is, Christ. " (Ephesians 4:14-15) Speak the truth, speak it lovingly, and grow more like Christ as you share your lives in accordance with Scripture.

Prayer for Today:

Dear God, it's easy to slip away from
following You completely or correctly. May I
depend on your Word for guidance above all
else. Please connect me with others so that we
can be a safety net for one another. Amen.

Rain, Rain, Go Away

But I tell you, love your enemies and pray for those who persecute you, that you may be children of your Father in heaven. He causes his sun to rise on the evil and the good, and sends rain on the righteous and the unrighteous. If you love those who love you, what reward will you get? Are not even the tax collectors doing that? Matthew 5:44-46

Tent camping on a rainy day quickly becomes tiresome. Avoiding mud puddles, trudging around in dripping ponchos, and attempting to keep the interior of the tent clean and dry - all of these experiences cause some to just pack up and head home early. Yet the rainy weekend we hope to avoid may be an answer to prayer for a farmer. It's interesting that while floods in the Bible are a symbol of the judgement of God, rain often represents God's blessing. "The Lord will open the heavens, the storehouse of his bounty, to send rain on your land in season and to bless all the work of your hands." (Deuteronomy 28:12) "Do any of the worthless idols of the nations bring rain? Do the skies themselves send down showers? No, it is you, Lord our God. Therefore our hope is in you, for you are the one who does all this." (Jeremiah 14:22)

If rain is indeed a blessing, then a well known verse from the Book of Matthew takes on a deeper meaning: "He causes his sun to rise on the evil and the good, and sends rain on the

25

righteous and the unrighteous." (Matthew 5:45) God's provision of rain is part of what theologians call "common grace", which includes the gifts that all humans receive from God, as well as God's restraining hand that prevents evil from totally overtaking the world. This verse is found in the context of Christ's teaching regarding loving and praying for our enemies. Such a hard thing to do! It's so much easier to love and pray for those who will love us in return. But Jesus said, "If you love those who love you, what reward will you get? Are not even the tax collectors doing that?" (Matthew 5:46) It's simply not appropriate to pat ourselves on the back for loving the lovely. If God sends drought-quenching showers to every sort of human being, we must love the most unlovely and pray for them to find life-changing forgiveness in Christ.

Prayer for Today:

Dear God, You send rain on the just and the unjust. You love the unlovely and desire for them to find salvation in You. May I not spend all my time with those who love me, and may I demonstrate grace toward all people, for your glory. Amen.

Sandal Straps

*John answered them all, "I baptize you with water. But one who is
more powerful than I will come, the straps of whose sandals I am not
worthy to untie."* Luke 3:16

Sandals designed for outdoor activities are usually
adjustable with hook and loop closures. In Bible days, the
soles of sandals were made from leather or wood, and the
straps were made from narrow leather bands. When a person
of influence entered a home, a servant would often be asked to
wash the dirty, dusty feet of the visitor, but the visitor would
take off their own sandals. Even servants or slaves were not
asked to perform that task. So when John says that he is not
worthy to untie the sandal straps of the Messiah, this illustrates
his awareness of the striking difference in both position and
holiness between himself and the coming Savior. John
demonstrates deep humility, despite the fact that he has become
rather well known and scores of people have come to him for
baptism.

Humility is a virtue that is rare in any time or culture, but
especially hard to find today. While it is proper to affirm that
every person has intrinsic worth because they have been
created by God, an inflated view of oneself in comparison to
others, and especially in comparison to God, is not consistent
with the teachings of Scripture. Job was reminded by God of
the Lord's greatness in verse after verse of the Book of Job:

27

"Where were you when I laid the earth's foundation? Tell me, if you understand. Who marked off its dimensions?" (Job 38:4-5) "Can you raise your voice to the clouds and cover yourself with a flood of water? Do you send the lightning bolts on their way? Do they report to you, 'Here we are'?" (Job 38:34-35)

Paul reminded the believers at Philippi, "Do nothing out of selfish ambition or vain conceit. Rather, in humility value others above yourselves, not looking to your own interests but each of you to the interests of the others." (Philippians 2:3-4) To the Colossians, he wrote, "Therefore, as God's chosen people, holy and dearly loved, clothe yourselves with compassion, kindness, humility, gentleness and patience." (Colossians 3:12)

The rewards of humility are many. "Humility is the fear of the Lord; its wages are riches and honor and life." (Proverbs 22:4) "All of you, clothe yourselves with humility toward one another, because, 'God opposes the proud but shows favor to the humble.'" (1 Peter 5:5)

Prayer for Today:

Dear God, You are the awesome, eternal
Creator. immeasurably far above me in power,
wisdom, and holiness. It does not bring honor
to You when I lack humility and am
exclusively absorbed with my own concerns
and interests. May I live as a humble and
grateful servant of yours today. Amen.

Go with the Flow

When we put bits into the mouths of horses to make them obey us, we can turn the whole animal. Or take ships as an example. Although they are so large and are driven by strong winds, they are steered by a very small rudder wherever the pilot wants to go. Likewise, the tongue is a small part of the body, but it makes great boasts. Consider what a great forest is set on fire by a small spark. James 3:3-5

Do you prefer kayaking, canoeing, or tubing? Floating down a river in a tube can be fun on a hot day if you are willing to have most of your body in the water and are not bothered by the lack of control you will have over your path down the river. You have to literally "go with the flow" of the current. A kayak or a canoe provides the opportunity for greater mastery over your direction if you properly use a paddle. The Book of James includes a similar nautical reference to describe the power that the tongue can have over human behavior, usually in a negative way. "Or take ships as an example. Although they are so large and are driven by strong winds, they are steered by a very small rudder." (James 3:4) James goes on to describe the tongue as a fire, a poison, and an untamable creature. Not a very positive portrait!

There are so many times in life when we wish that we could take back something we have just blurted out. We can apologize, but often the damage to a situation or a relationship can be hard to mend. Proverbs 13:3 warns, "Those who guard their lips preserve their lives, but those who speak rashly will come to ruin." Proverbs 29:20 states, "Do you see someone who speaks in haste? There is more hope for a fool than for them."

So how can I avoid letting my tongue lead me aimlessly down a river of misery? How can I use my tongue as a rudder for good? First, I must spend more time listening more than speaking. "Everyone should be quick to listen, slow to speak and slow to become angry." (James 1:19) This is even more important when approaching the Almighty. "Do not be quick with your mouth, do not be hasty in your heart to utter anything before God. God is in heaven and you are on earth, so let your words be few." (Ecclesiastes 5:2) Next, ask God to purify your heart from within. "For the mouth speaks what the heart is full of." (Matthew 12:34) Finally, pray for self-control. "Set a guard over my mouth, LORD; keep watch over the door of my lips." (Psalm 141:3)

Prayer for Today:

Dear God, I agree with the psalmist in Psalm
19:14: "May these words of my mouth and
this meditation of my heart be pleasing in your
sight, LORD, my Rock and my Redeemer."
Amen.

Unmentionables

For you were once darkness, but now you are light in the Lord. Live as children of light (for the fruit of the light consists in all goodness, righteousness, and truth) and find out what pleases the Lord. Have nothing to do with the fruitless deeds of darkness, but rather expose them. It is shameful even to mention what the disobedient do in secret.
Ephesians 5:8-12

At the end of every troop campout, my Girl Scout leader would collect a box of gear and clothing that had been left behind at the campsite. She would bring the box to the next regular Scout meeting, holding up each item that needed to be claimed. "Whose flashlight is this? How about this cat T-shirt?" Often the final item would be a pair of panties, and she would say, "And now we have a pair of unmentionables." Giggles would ensue, and the owner would have to endure some teasing in order to claim her lingerie. There's nothing inherently shameful about a pair of underwear, but it would be easy to feel ashamed to have one's secret items mentioned in public.

Over time, our society has lost some of its sense of shame over certain public actions, such as the flippant use of God's name and open boasting of habits that don't honor the Lord. Paul told the Ephesian believers that disobedient acts committed in secret are shameful even to be mentioned aloud. That statement may seem heavy-handed, but it actually makes sense when you look at the context. Paul is not speaking to the world at large; he is speaking to the church. He has already reminded them that the darkness of their former lives has been changed to light, evidenced by goodness, righteousness, and truth. He states that the natural result of the radical change in our lives should be to seek the things that please the Lord. Obedience should overflow from thankfulness for all that He has done for us. Paul also wants the Ephesians to remember that the deeds of darkness are fruitless, another word for ineffective, and he urges them to avoid those deeds completely.

It's not likely that we will be able to change the surrounding culture's pride in actions and attitudes that should be considered unmentionable. But we can ask God to make us aware when we begin to gradually adopt those same habits. Goodness, righteousness, and truth should be our hallmarks. The ultimate goal is not to jump through behavioral hoops grudgingly, but to wholeheartedly and joyfully seek to please the Lord in all that we think, say, and do.

Prayer for Today:

Dear God, you have brought me from darkness
into your marvelous light. Help me to reject
anything that is of the dark, purifying my
attitudes, thoughts, and actions out of grateful
devotion to You. May my life honor You this
day.   Amen.

Fools and Bears

Better to meet a bear robbed of her cubs than a fool bent on folly.
Proverbs 17:12

When hiking in bear country, there are a number of ways to protect yourself. Some hikers carry bear spray, while others hike in groups and talk loudly among themselves as they go down the trail. (I prefer singing!) It's also helpful to double bag your food, pack out all food and trash, and avoid wearing earbuds so that you can be more aware of your surroundings. Look for fresh tracks and scat left behind by bears, and never get between a mother bear and her offspring.

The Book of Proverbs says that it is better to meet a bear robbed of her cubs than to encounter a foolish person that is determined to continue in their folly. Folly does not merely mean poorly considered ideas. Some synonyms for *folly* are *idiocy, lunacy, madness,* and *stupidity.* The opposite of *folly* is *wisdom* and *discernment.* We are advised to avoid the foolish, so what are some characteristics of a foolish person?

* "The fool says in his heart, 'There is no God.'" (Psalm 14:1) Fools deny the existence of God or live as if He has no authority to rule over their lives.

* "Rise up, O God, and defend your cause; remember how fools mock you all day long." (Psalm 74:22) Fools speak contemptuously about God.
* "The fear of the Lord is the beginning of knowledge, but fools despise wisdom and instruction." (Proverbs 1:7) Fools are unwilling to accept wise directives.
* "The wise in heart accept commands, but a chattering fool comes to ruin." (Proverbs 10:8) Fools often talk too much.
* "The way of fools seems right to them, but the wise listen to advice." (Proverbs 12:15) Fools think they always know best.
* "Fools find no pleasure in understanding but delight in airing their own opinions." (Proverbs 18:2) Fools enjoy spouting out their opinions to others.
* "Do not be quickly provoked in your spirit, for anger resides in the lap of fools." (Ecclesiastes 7:9) Fools have a short fuse.
* "Walk with the wise and become wise, for a companion of fools suffers harm." (Proverbs 13:20) Hanging around with fools leads to harmful consequences.

Prayer for Today:

Dear Lord, I don't like to think of myself as being foolish, but I know that sometimes I display the characteristics of a fool. Help me to be a good listener, to accept wise instruction, to control my temper, and to honor your name. Show me if I need to step back from the company of someone in my life, and grant me discernment along every path. Amen.

What Do You See?

Don't you have a saying, "It's still four months until harvest"? I tell you, open your eyes and look at the fields! They are ripe for harvest. Even now the one who reaps draws a wage and harvests a crop for eternal life, so that the sower and the reaper may be glad together. Thus the saying "One sows and another reaps" is true. John 4:35-37

Whenever I hike on a difficult trail that leads to an overlook, I remind myself that only those who put in the hard work of climbing will be able to enjoy the amazing view. But how about the creatures that are native to that spot? They have the opportunity to be a part of that idyllic scene every single day. We can only guess whether or not those animals have an appreciation for what they view, but I would hope that I never cease to truly see the beauty of God's amazing creation.

On the very day that Jesus revealed himself as the Messiah to the Samaritan woman, he reminded his disciples to look around and notice that many are ready even now to believe in Him. Although the woman was a member of an ethnic group that the Jews despised, and though she was ostracized by many in her town because of her lifestyle, she accepted Christ's message and immediately ran back into the village to tell anyone who would listen about his identity. Her belief and

35

enthusiasm resulted in the salvation of many Samaritans from that town. Jesus knew that the Samaritan village was ripe for the harvest.

Looking at strangers around me as I shop or travel, I rarely truly notice these people as individuals for whom Christ gave his life, individuals who may be ready to hear a message of hope, forgiveness, and eternal life. I am often too absorbed in my phone or my mental "to do" list to pay attention to individuals and their needs. But Jesus commands us to open our eyes. We may fulfill the role of a sower, putting forth a gentle encouragement or challenge relating to our faith. We may be a reaper who helps someone take their final steps into true belief. Both sower and reaper are to be glad together. If we don't take Jesus at his word that many are ready to hear about Him, our reluctance to get involved in the lives of others will leave those individuals still searching for meaning and will leave ourselves without the joy of being used by our Lord.

"I tell you, open your eyes and look at the fields! They are ripe for harvest." (John 4:35)

Prayer for Today:

Dear God, open my eyes! Make me sensitive to the needs of those around me, even strangers. I do not have the words that are needed, but You will help me if I will just be obedient. May everything that I say be spoken in love, and may I listen more than I speak. Amen.

Money Back Guarantee

Now it is God who makes both us and you stand firm in Christ. He anointed us, set his seal of ownership on us, and put his Spirit in our hearts as a deposit, guaranteeing what is to come.
2 Corinthians 1:21-22

A money back guarantee is a wonderful sales promise that can really increase your willingness to pay for an expensive piece of camping equipment. Many companies put a time limit or coverage limit on their promise, so the guarantee becomes a limited warranty. And of course there are those annoying sales pitches for extended warranties. ("This recreational vehicle is amazing, but you should buy an extended warranty just in case it's not...")

The Bible speaks of a guaranteed inheritance, a promise of future eternal spiritual blessings. "And you also were included in Christ when you heard the message of truth, the gospel of your salvation. When you believed, you were marked in him with a seal, the promised Holy Spirit, who is a deposit guaranteeing our inheritance until the redemption of those who are God's possession - to the praise of his glory." (Ephesians 1:13-14) It's not a money back guarantee because this inheritance was never purchased by us, but rather by the precious blood of Christ in his sacrifice for us on the cross.

"For you know that it was not with perishable things such as silver or gold that you were redeemed…but with the precious blood of Christ." (1 Peter 1:18-19) But it is a certain guarantee, because God always fulfills his promises.

We belong to Him, and nothing can ever separate us from his love. "For I am convinced that neither death nor life, neither angels nor demons, neither the present nor the future, nor any powers, neither height nor depth, nor anything else in all creation, will be able to separate us from the love of God that is in Christ Jesus our Lord." (Romans 8:38-39). Paul told both the Corinthian and the Ephesian believers that the Holy Spirit living in our hearts would act as a seal or deposit that ensures we will receive this promised inheritance. Our guarantee is freely extended through every year of our life and into eternity. Thanks be to God!

Prayer for Today:

Dear God, only You have the power to back up
your promises. Because I have believed in
Christ and have accepted your free gift of
salvation, I can never be separated from your
love. Your Holy Spirit assures me that I will
inherit many spiritual blessings now, and
eternal life in the future. Thank you so much
for this amazing guarantee, and help me to
gratefully live for You. Amen.

Support System

The eternal God is your refuge, and underneath are the everlasting arms. Deuteronomy 33:27

Kings Canyon National Park is filled with amazing vistas, but there is only one driving route into the canyon. The Kings Canyon Scenic Byway includes steep elevation changes, numerous sharp turns, and almost no guard rails. All in all it can be a rather terrifying journey, although the views are incredible once you stop at an overlook. It is the scarcity of guard rails that creates the most tension for me, the knowledge that one false move could send the car plummeting down a cliff.

Scientific studies have shown that when young children play on a playground that is fenced, they utilize all of the available play space. The children feel relaxed, confident, and more free to explore. When there are no visible boundaries, the kids tend to huddle close to their teachers. In the same way, children whose parents set consistent behavioral boundaries are more easygoing and assured, because they know what to expect from day to day.

God has given us guidelines in the Bible for our joy and protection. "Jumping the guard rail" doesn't normally lead to greater happiness. But what about those areas in life for which there are no clear Scriptural directions? "If any of you lacks wisdom, you should ask God, who gives generously to all without finding fault, and it will be given to you." (James 1:5) If we get off the correct road, God offers forgiveness. "If we confess our sins, he is faithful and just and will forgive us our sins and purify us from all unrighteousness." (1 John 1:9)

What can we do during times of sickness, family difficulties, or confusion, when we feel as though we are teetering near a cliff's edge? Isaiah 41:10 offers a reassuring promise: "So do not fear, for I am with you; do not be dismayed, for I am your God. I will strengthen you and help you; I will uphold you with my righteous right hand." (Isaiah 41:10) Jesus promised that He would always be with us, no matter the situation. "And surely I am with you always, to the very end of the age" (Matthew 28:20)

Like the wise parent, God is consistent in both his expectations and his faithfulness. Like a sturdy guard rail, God will always be there to uphold and strengthen us. "The eternal God is your refuge, and underneath are the everlasting arms." (Deuteronomy 33:27)

Prayer for Today:

Dear Lord, you are the same yesterday, today, and forever. The truth in your Word will never change. Thank you that living in your truth will be for my good and for your glory, and thank you that You encourage and help me when I cannot support myself. Amen.

I Just Want to Be with You

When they saw the courage of Peter and John and realized that they were unschooled, ordinary men, they were astonished and they took note that these men had been with Jesus. Acts 4:13

Road trips with children can be challenging. My parents tried to avoid traffic and restless kids by leaving the house around 4:00 AM. The idea was that the children would groggily walk to the car, buckle up, and then immediately fall back asleep for the next several hours. Because this was the era before child safety seats, my normal spot in the station wagon as the youngest child was the center section of a front bench seat, sandwiched between my parents. Although my father was an Air Force pilot and was well practiced in staying alert at all hours, I felt that it was my duty to keep him awake for the first part of the trip. I'm not sure how much he appreciated my incessant chatter, but I expect he enjoyed knowing that I wanted to hang out with him.

In ancient Israel, a disciple would literally follow his teacher wherever he went. Not only would he listen to the teacher's instructions, but he would learn a great deal about life by watching the master in everyday situations. There was as much spiritual formation "caught" as taught. How can we learn from the master today? Reading through the Gospels (the

41

New Testament books Matthew, Mark, Luke, and John) multiple times is a good way to start. In your first reading, focus on who Jesus claimed to be, his miracles, and his teachings. Read the books a second time, looking specifically at the way Jesus reacts to the same sorts of negative situations that we often encounter: opposition, betrayal by friends, misunderstanding of his message. The third time, concentrate on how Jesus demonstrates the fruit of the Sprit: "love, joy, peace, forbearance, kindness, goodness faithfulness". (Galatians 5:22) In addition to reading the Scriptures to learn from Jesus, we can also draw close to him in humble prayer.

The lives of the early disciples were gradually transformed during the three years when they literally followed Jesus. An even greater transformation occurred as they encountered the risen Christ and as the promised Holy Spirit came to indwell and empower them. Those who interacted with the disciples noticed their boldness: "When they saw the courage of Peter and John and realized that they were unschooled, ordinary men, they were astonished and they took note that these men had been with Jesus." (Acts 4:13) Oh, that our lives would be marked by love and by faithfulness to the teachings of Christ, a reflection of the time spent with Jesus!

Prayer for Today:

Dear Jesus, I want to be your disciple and learn
from you. As I read the Gospels, make your
ways clear to me, and may your Word change
my life. Amen.

Nature's Garbage Collectors

Wherever there is a carcass, there the vultures will gather.
Matthew 24:28

Vultures get a bad rap! Normally, they are pictured feasting on a dead animal, and this disgusts our sensibilities. But they are beautiful in flight, soaring with outstretched wings. Untrained observers are likely to confuse a vulture with a graceful hawk. In addition, vultures serve an essential purpose as one of the "garbage collectors" or scavengers of the food web. Scavengers aid in the decomposition process that returns nutrients to the soil. Vultures are well suited to their unpopular job because they have a strong sense of sight and smell. Their talons aren't very strong, but they don't need brawny talons since they do not hunt. God perfectly designed the vulture for its purpose in life.

In his first letter to the church at Corinth, Paul addresses some problems and divisions among that group of believers. One issue was that certain individuals considered themselves to be followers of Paul, while others followed Apollos (another early church teacher.) In the letter, Paul does not make a grab for the loyalty of all; rather, he reminds them that both he and Apollos have the same ultimate purpose: "What, after all, is Apollos? And what is Paul? Only servants, through whom you came to believe-as the Lord has assigned to each his task. I planted the seed, Apollos watered it, but God has been making it grow...The one who plants and the one who waters have one purpose, and they will each be rewarded according to their own labor. For we are co-workers in God's service." (1 Corinthians 3:5-6, 8-9) Paul and Apollos had different gifts and responsibilities, both perfectly suited to their contribution to a common purpose.

If there is a pastor or spiritual mentor that you especially like, it's acceptable to tell others about that person's positive qualities. But it's not a good idea to push our preferences in leadership upon others. Even the most godly or eloquent leader is an imperfect human, and God has uniquely created leaders with many different styles and skills that will appeal to a variety of people. In addition, at one point in our spiritual journey there may be a person who reaches out to us, planting a seed, but a different person may be the one who "waters" our initial bit of faith. Both of these people need your prayers and support in order to fulfill the purpose that God has for them.

Prayer for Today:

Dear God, may I remember that your servants
on Earth are not perfect, and may I never be
overbearing in my praise of any human. Thank
you for the mentors who have cared about me
and have helped me to draw closer to You.
Thank you for giving them special skills, and
help them to faithfully teach your Word and
live according to the truth. Amen.

Rubs Me the Wrong Way

So when you, a mere human being, pass judgment on them and yet do the same things, do you think you will escape God's judgment? Or do you show contempt for the riches of his kindness, forbearance and patience, not realizing that God's kindness is intended to lead you to repentance? Romans 2:3-4

Breaking in a new pair of hiking boots needs to be a gradual process in order to avoid blisters. It can take a few wearings for the boots to conform to your feet and for your feet to toughen up in those areas that are sliding across your skin at a new angle. A moleskin bandage might also be necessary to cushion the tender areas for a period of time. But what can I do when a certain person "rubs me the wrong way", sometimes for reasons that I can't even articulate?

First, I have to remind myself that not everyone shares my opinions or personality traits. My father used to say, "That's why they make Fords and Chevrolets." Next, I must remember that God has been patient with me. "Bear with each other and forgive one another if any of you has a grievance against someone. Forgive as the Lord forgave you." (Colossians 3:13) In addition, compassion and love can allow me to look past the irritating habits of others. "The Lord is compassionate and gracious, slow to anger, abounding in love." (Psalm 103:8)

Finally, it can be true that we share in some way the habits that so irritate us when we observe them in others. "If we claim to be without sin, we deceive ourselves and the truth is not in us. If we confess our sins, he is faithful and just and will forgive us our sins and purify us from all unrighteousness." (1 John 1:8-10)

Have you ever imagined what it was like for the twelve disciples to travel and work together? Although some of them (like Peter and Andrew) were brothers, most of the men were strangers before being called by Jesus. They came from a wide variety of professions and had very different personalities. At times, the men argued about which one of them was the greatest, and they doubtless had many other disagreements. Yet Jesus specifically chose each member of the group for reasons known only to himself. After the resurrection of Christ, they were able to "turn the world upside down" as they worked together to share the good news of the risen Lord.

Prayer for Today:

Dear Lord, there are so many people in the world that I find it hard to get along with, even within your family of believers. Help me to have a patient spirit and the heart of a peacemaker. May I not judge others when I have so many faults of my own. I want to be loving so that all will know that I truly follow You. Amen.

Take Peace Along for the Ride

Peace I leave with you; my peace I give you. I do not give to you as the world gives. Do not let your hearts be troubled and do not be afraid.
John 14:27

It has well been said that wherever you go, you carry yourself along. Traveling to humble or exotic destinations makes no difference. Just as physical limitations can prevent us from accessing certain trails that others are able to enjoy, feelings of worry and depression can sit like a weight, robbing us from true relaxation. Fearful, troubled hearts can only be changed by an inner peace that comes from Jesus.

Christ promised his peace just after assuring the disciples that the Holy Spirit would come to them after his resurrection. "All this I have spoken while still with you. But the Advocate, the Holy Spirit, whom the Father will send in my name, will teach you all things and will remind you of everything I have said to you. Peace I leave with you; my peace I give you." (John 14:25-27) Using this passage, let's explore how the Spirit can bring peace:

- The Spirit comes from the Father. He is our loving God who cares for us and has the power to help us in our time of need.

47

- The Spirit is our teacher. We often lack wisdom, but the Spirit can grant insight.
- The Spirit will remind us of truths spoken by Jesus. Of course, we have to take the initiative to study the Bible, but Christ can remind us daily of what we have learned, bringing encouragement and strength. It's also important to note that the Holy Spirit assisted the Biblical writers, helping them to remember and accurately record of the words of Christ.
- Peace from the Spirit does not follow the pattern of peace that comes from the world. The world's peace is totally dependent on external circumstances. God's peace is internal and flows from confidence in the goodness and power of God.
- The Spirit is our Advocate. An advocate is similar to legal counsel. Synonyms for *advocate* include *attorney, supporter, champion,* and *counselor.* The Spirit stands up for us and takes charge of our defense.

Prayer for Today:

Dear Lord, You promised peace through the indwelling of the Holy Spirit that lives inside every believer. Help me to trust in your love and your omnipotence. Please bring to my mind and heart daily the truth that is found in your Word. May your peace take hold of me and change me from within. Amen.

Hidden Hues

But who can discern their own errors? Forgive my hidden faults.
Psalm 19:12

Autumn is a favorite season for many campers because of the spectacle of vivid colors in the fall leaves. It's common to say that the leaves are "changing colors", but science tells us that most of the bright pigments have been a part of the leaves throughout the spring and summer. The colorful hues have been masked by green pigments contained in chlorophyl, a chemical that is necessary for the plant to make its own food. When temperatures cool and the hours of daylight decrease, the chlorophyll breaks down and the autumn colors become visible.

In a similar way, the inner character of each person is a mixture of worthy and unworthy thoughts, attitudes, and desires. It's easy to excuse our inner faults that we are conscious of, especially if our outer behavior generally aligns with the accepted customs of society, even with the expectations of the church. And what about the character shortcomings that we don't even recognize? The psalmist wrote, "who can discern their own errors? Forgive my hidden faults." (Psalm 19:12) Whether our faults are hidden or lingering at the edges of our consciousness, how can anyone make a deliberate plan to eradicate them?

- Decide that you truly want to be aware of inner faults that displease God. Apathy will not lead to any real change.
- Read Psalm 139, which reminds us in detail of how completely God knows us.
- Prayerfully ask God to open your eyes to the true state of your heart. "Search me, God and know my heart…" (Psalm 139:23)
- Remember that God loves you deeply, and don't despair if you have setbacks on this journey.
- Recognize that the power to change comes from our salvation through Christ. "Therefore, if anyone is in Christ, the new creation has come: The old has gone, the new is here!" (2 Corinthians 5:17)
- Trust in the faithfulness of God. "If we confess our sins, he is faithful and just and will forgive us our sins and purify us from all unrighteousness." (1 John 1:9)

Prayer for Today:

Dear God, I come to You, seeking to know the true state of my heart. Thank you that You know everything about me and are still filled with love towards me. Please show me the changes that I need to make in my attitudes and thoughts. Only your power can make me pure within. Amen.

The Splendor of the Stars

He is the Maker of the Bear and Orion, the Pleiades and the constellations of the south. Job 9:9
The sun has one kind of splendor, the moon another and the stars another; and star differs from star in splendor. 1 Corinthians 15:41

Constellations are groups of stars that seem to form patterns, based on our perspective from Earth. Certain stars within a constellation may appear close to one another, but in reality they may be many light-years apart. Ancient peoples created stories about the star patterns because the predictable movements of the constellations helped them mark the seasons for planting and harvesting. But even if star stories are man-made, God has always been the Maker of the stars.

In 1 Corinthians chapter fifteen, Paul writes a detailed argument for the resurrection of the physical bodies of believers at the second coming of Christ. He first compares this process to that of a seed being planted and then growing into a living thing that has a very different form from the original seed. "When you sow, you do not plant the body that will be, but just a seed…So will it be with the resurrection of the dead. The body that is sown is perishable, it is raised imperishable." (1 Corinthians 15:37, 42) He then explains that just as different stars have different kinds of splendor, our resurrected bodies will have a different form than our earthly

51

bodies. "There are also heavenly bodies and there are earthly bodies...The sun has one kind of splendor, the moon another and the stars another; and star differs from star in splendor... Listen, I tell you a mystery: We will not all sleep, but we will all be changed-in a flash, in the twinkling of an eye, at the last trumpet. For the trumpet will sound, the dead will be raised imperishable, and we will be changed...Where, O death, is your victory? (1 Corinthians 15:40, 41, 51, 52, 55) Death does not have any ultimate power over us as believers in Christ.

If we die before the return of Jesus, our bodies will be raised into imperishable bodies when the trumpet signals his coming. What if we are alive at that moment? "After that, we who are still alive and are left will be caught up together with them in the clouds to meet the Lord in the air. And so we will be with the Lord forever. Therefore encourage one another with these words." (1 Thessalonians 4:17-18). This is not just some "pie in the sky" fairy tale. The God who wove through the Old Testament hundreds of prophesies about the first coming of Christ, all of which were fulfilled, is the same God who has promised that Jesus will return. The second coming of Christ is an event to anticipate with joy! Think of his return whenever you gaze at the splendor of the stars.

Prayer for Today:
Dear Jesus, You were one with the Father when the stars were created. Every prophecy concerning your time on Earth came true, and every prophecy about your return will surely come to pass. Thank you for the beauty of the stars and the predictability of the constellations. How awesome and faithful You are! Amen.

One Generation Away

After that whole generation had been gathered to their ancestors, another generation arose who knew neither the Lord nor what he had done for Israel. Judges 2:10

At one point in my life, I thought that a dream job would be that of a park ranger. I could visualize myself in a green and khaki uniform, teaching kids about nature, maintaining trails, and preventing forest fires, all in breathtaking settings. Unfortunately, that career path can also have its drawbacks: relatively low pay, serving at the whim of potential government budget cuts, working almost every weekend, and living far from extended family and social activities. But if you are well suited to these working conditions, you will gain the satisfaction of serving as a guardian of special areas of natural splendor and historical significance, preserving these lands for future generations to enjoy. Without specific preservation, the beauty and peacefulness of the parks would quickly become overrun by commercial development and pollution, lost forever to the next generation.

Our spiritual heritage is also a single generation from extinction. The Old Testament is filled with numerous accounts of kings and entire nations who turned away from the true God of their elders and began to practice idolatry. The book of Judges speaks specifically of those who witnessed the fall of the walls of Jericho, the miracles in the wilderness, and the drying up of the Jordan River. When that generation died, the next generation did not make the faith of their fathers their own personal faith. Somehow, the accounts of the awesome deeds of God and the committed belief of those who had witnessed those deeds had not been passed on. How can this be avoided?

Prayer is obviously essential, remembering to pray for our children, grandchildren, and the little ones in our sphere of influence, asking God to work in their lives. It's also important to verbalize some specific ways that God has been real to us. The young ones in the next generation need to understand that God is not a vague idea, but a personal, real part of our daily struggles and joys. Don't rely on pastors to fill this role of recounting the goodness and power of the Lord. Let those coming behind us sense that following and serving God is an amazing, exciting, fulfilling privilege.

Prayer for Today:

Dear God, help me to live for You in such a way that those who come after me will want to follow and serve You. Give me boldness to share the difference that You have made in my life. Let me pass along the truths of your Word in humility and love. Amen.

As Good as I Get

Charm is deceptive, and beauty is fleeting, but a woman who fears the Lord is to be praised. Proverbs 31:30

A backpacking trip is not a time to worry about appearances. It's much more important to choose layers of clothing that will work well in a variety of weather scenarios than to make a fashion statement. Even if a woman buys designer camping clothing from the most trendy retailers, there's the problem of carrying along the unnecessary weight of beauty products, not to mention the lack of mirrors. It's best to just accept that when camping, "This is as good as I get."

But what about my inner character? It's very easy to be satisfied with my inner motives, thoughts, and attitudes - the part of me that is only seen by God. I can make excuses for my feelings of envy and dissatisfaction. I can fail to honestly view my own lack of desire to grow in holiness. Popular wisdom tells me that I must learn to love myself, and that is true to some degree. But it's also important to recognize those areas of my character that need refining. How much more could I be used by God if my goals, reasoning, and perspectives were honoring to Christ?

The road to inner change has several steps. First, I need to ask forgiveness for those things that I have been aware of, but have stubbornly refused to address. "But with you there is forgiveness, so that we can, with reverence, serve you." (Psalm 130:4) Next, I should ask God to enable me to make the changes that I can't make for myself. "If we confess our sins, he is faithful and just and will forgive us our sins and purify us from all unrighteousness." (1 John 1:9) Finally, I can be shaped into a more godly person by consistently reading the Scriptures. "I delight in your decrees, I will not neglect your word." (Psalm 119:16)

Prayer for Today:

Dear God, you know all about me, and your
desire is for me to be more and more like your
Son, the Lord Jesus Christ. May I not look for
excuses when You have given me your Holy
Spirit to change me from the inside. Let me
listen to your voice as You speak to me through
the Bible, and help me to be obedient today.
Amen.

A Joyful Noise

David told the leaders of the Levites to appoint their fellow Levites as musicians to make a joyful sound with musical instruments: lyres, harps and cymbals. 1 Chronicles 15:16
Shout for joy to the Lord, all the earth, burst into jubilant song with music. Psalm 98:4
Let the rivers clap their hands, let the mountains sing together for joy. Psalm 98:8

The "joyful noise" of some people around the campfire is a bit subdued because they don't have confidence in their singing ability. Yet many Bible verses that mention singing with joy are pretty exuberant, using words like *shout* and *jubilant* and mentioning boisterous instruments such as cymbals.

When the wind rustles through the trees, it creates a lovely sound. We know that all of creation was designed to bring glory to God, and many portions of Scripture describe the creation as joyfully singing the praises of God. It's wonderful to consider that humans and nature can both share in the experience of joyously bringing honor and glory to God. "Clap your hands, all you nations; shout to God with cries of joy." (Psalm 47:1) "Let the fields be jubilant, and everything in them; let all the trees of the forest sing for joy." (Psalm 96:12) "The whole earth is filled with awe at your wonders; where morning dawns, where evening fades, you call forth songs of joy." (Psalm 65:8)

The people of Zion were so renowned for their upbeat singing that when they were carried away into captivity, their captors mocked them by demanding that they sing joyfully. "There on the poplars we hung our harps, for there our captors asked us for songs, our tormentors demanded songs of joy; they said, 'Sing us one of the songs of Zion!'" (Psalm 137:2-3) Is my life equally characterized by joy? The Holy Spirit lives within each believer, so my attitude should reflect the Spirit's qualities: "the fruit of the Spirit is love, joy, peace, forbearance, kindness, goodness, faithfulness, gentleness, and self control." (Galatians 5:22-23)

Prayer for Today:

Dear God, over and over your Word reminds us
to exuberantly express joyful praise to You.
May my words, songs, even my facial
expressions and my thoughts be marked by
overflowing joy. Amen.

So Annoying

Now if the foot should say, "Because I am not a hand, I do not belong to the body," it would not for that reason stop being part of the body. And if the ear should say, "Because I am not an eye, I do not belong to the body," it would not for that reason stop being part of the body…Now you are the body of Christ, and each one of you is a part of it.
1 Corinthians 12:15, 16. 27

It's always a good idea to check your tent area for roots, rocks, and other protrusions before setting up camp. Even a single stone or stick can cause a camper to identify with the princess in the fairy tale *The Princess and the Pea*. This princess was said to be so delicate that even a tiny pea under a stack of mattresses caused her to toss and turn all night. Similarly, a pebble inside your hiking boot can cause annoyance or outright pain.

Do you know an acquaintance, neighbor, or fellow club member who has a habit or mannerism that is an underlying irritation for you? A strange laugh or a way of speaking, a different way of approaching group tasks - nothing illegal or immoral, but somehow that quirk just gets on your nerves. When I really consider this, it occurs to me that I probably have equally annoying idiosyncrasies of which I am totally unaware. It's not reasonable to expect everyone to share my opinions, preferences, and ways of speaking or working.

Paul reminds the Corinthian church in 1 Corinthians 12 that different members of the spiritual body have different roles. We can't all have the role of the eye or take the position of the foot. Each person has different strengths, so we shouldn't want or expect others to be like us. The body only works when each part fulfills its role (a good reminder that we shouldn't sit on the sidelines and expect 10% of the people to do 90% of the work.) We also shouldn't expect the personalities and habits of others to fit our own preferences. If the other person is living according to God's Word and not disrupting the unity of the group, we may need to overlook some minor issues that annoy us. Finally, we can look honestly and critically at ourselves to see if some of our actions or habits could be classified as abrasive, distracting, or tiresome.

Prayer for Today:

Dear God, please help me to view myself truthfully. Show me any parts of my life that do not honor You, and help me to get rid of mannerisms, speech, and actions that would push others away from your truth. May all that I think, say, and do be guided by love. When I find others to be annoying, grant me patience and grace. Help every part of your body, the church, to do their part and work together in harmony for the advancement of your kingdom on Earth. Amen.

A Good Investment

My goal is that they may be encouraged in heart and united in love, so that they may have the full richness of complete understanding, in order that they may know the mystery of God, namely, Christ, in whom are hidden all the treasures of wisdom and knowledge. Colossians 2: 2-3

High quality camping gear is expensive! It can be difficult to fork over the money required to purchase items that are well made, but the investment will pay off if those items last for many years. Scrimping on the quality of your gear can lead to a hole in your boot sole when you are halfway through your hike, a jammed zipper on your parka in 40 degree weather, or water leaking into your tent at 3:00 AM.

Would you be willing to invest in wisdom and knowledge? "Blessed are those who find wisdom, those who gain understanding." (Proverbs 3:13) The Bible says that wisdom and knowledge are treasures that can be found in Christ. "Christ, in whom are hidden all the treasures of wisdom and knowledge." (Colossians 2:3) The benefits are many. "Do not forsake wisdom, and she will protect you". (Proverbs 4:6) "Blessed is the one who heeds wisdom's instruction." (Proverbs 29:18) How can we cultivate these treasures in our lives?

- Remember that life is brief: "Teach us to number our days, that we may gain a heart of wisdom." (Psalm 90:12)
- Live in awe before God: "The fear of the Lord is the beginning of wisdom". (Psalm 111:10) "The fear of the Lord is the beginning of knowledge, but fools despise wisdom and instruction." (Proverbs 1:7)
- Desire wisdom above the other goals in your life: "for wisdom is more precious than rubies, and nothing you desire can compare with her." (Proverbs 8:11)
- Ask God for wisdom and knowledge, and use God's Word as your guide: "If any of you lacks wisdom, you should ask God, who gives generously to all without finding fault, and it will be given to you." (James 1:5) "Teach me knowledge and good judgement, for I trust your commands" (Psalm 119:66)
- Do not boast in the knowledge that you obtain: "If I have the gift of prophecy and can fathom all mysteries and all knowledge, and if I have a faith that can move mountains, but do not have love, I am nothing." (1 Corinthians 13:2)
-

Prayer for Today:

Dear God, I need wisdom and knowledge in
order to live for You each day. You are the
holy God, and I submit to your commands.
Thank you for the wise example of Christ and
for the indwelling Holy Spirit that will be my
guide. May all that I think, say, and do today
be marked by wisdom and love. Amen.

Lethal Stake

Sisera, the commander of his army, was based in Harosheth Haggoyim. Because he had nine hundred chariots fitted with iron and had cruelly oppressed the Israelites for twenty years, they cried to the Lord for help...Then Deborah said to Barak, "Go! This is the day the Lord has given Sisera into your hands...At Barak's advance, the Lord routed Sisera and all his chariots and army...Sisera, meanwhile, fled on food to the tent of Jael... "Stand in the doorway of the tent," he told her. "If someone comes by and asks you, 'Is anyone in there?' say 'No.'" But Jael, Heber's wife, picked up a tent peg and a hammer and went quietly to him while he lay fast asleep, exhausted. She drove the peg through his temple into the ground, and he died. Judges 4: 2-3, 14, 15, 17, 20-21*

Did you know that a tent stake plays an important role in an Old Testament Bible story? But this story is unlikely to be included in your toddler's Sunday School curriculum. Jael killed Sisera by driving a tent stake through Sisera's skull into the ground. Now that's an intense story! All the details can be found in the Book of Judges chapter four. What can we learn from this rather violent account that could possibly have any application for our lives today?

- The Israelites had turned away from the Lord by worshipping idols, so God allowed their nation to fall into the hands of Jabin, king of Canaan. There are real consequences to idolatry and disobedience. God will not be mocked.

- Sisera was Jabin's powerful military commander. He had many resources (900 chariots) and had cruelly oppressed God's people for 20 years. God knew that Sisera was not an innocent victim.
- Deborah , a prophet and Judge of Israel, instructed Barak to bring armed men from the tribes of Naphtali and Zebulun to Mount Tabor. She specifically and accurately prophesied that Sisera would be delivered into the hands of a woman and that Sisera's armies would be routed. God knows the future.
- Jael's husband was an ally of Jabin the cruel king. Jael was taking a huge risk by aligning herself with Barak and Deborah. God may call us to complete difficult tasks. We can't expect to live a life devoid of challenges, but God will be with us.
- Barak didn't demonstrate much boldness during his conversation with Deborah, so she informed him that a woman would be the one to take down Sisera. But he did eventually trust God enough to bring his troops into warfare with the stronger army of Sisera. In the New Testament, Barak's name is included in the "faith hall of fame" in Hebrews chapter 11. A lapse of faith does not have to be forever.

Prayer for Today:

Dear God, the characters in this Bible story were real individuals who had different levels of fear and faith. May I never turn away from You or idolize possessions or people. Forgive me for the times that I have not trusted or obeyed You. Please grant me boldness to serve You in difficult situations. Amen.

Silver and Gold

Offer hospitality to one another without grumbling. 1 Peter 4:9

Many of us remember sitting around a campfire with our Girl Scout buddies and singing, "Make new friends but keep the old; one is silver and the other gold." Others recall going camping with our family and striking up temporary friendships with other kids who were camping nearby. My mom taught me to just walk over and introduce myself, so pretty soon we would all be creating games with sticks or sharing whatever toys we had brought along on the trip. Nobody was concerned about race, religion, or political affiliation. As long as the family in the next campsite didn't curse up a storm or own a vicious-looking dog, it was fine for me to just amble over and start a conversation. So why is it so much harder as adults, at a campsite or in our neighborhood?

First, it's easy to spend so much time around people who are just like us that we forget how to make connections with those who are different. Just keep it simple and introduce yourself. You're not signing on for a lifetime relationship, only sharing your life and your hospitality. It's also easy to view cordiality as a practice only for extroverts. If you're an introvert, you may not be particularly interested in reaching out. But God wants people of every personality type to share the grace and hope of Jesus, and your peaceful demeanor may actually appeal to your neighbor.

In addition, our society doesn't encourage interaction with strangers (other than small talk about the weather.) When we have bits of spare time, it's just easier to look at our phone or to make contact with people that are already in our current circle of relationships. If we go through our days not even considering the possibility of reaching out, then those who are new to town, or those who are recovering from difficult situations, or those who will never have the courage to approach others can be left high and dry.

Finally, we often forget that a small moment of interaction can make a big difference in someone's life. "Random acts of kindness" can go a long way. A sincere compliment, an offer of help, or a shared item can provide a moment of encouragement or become the first step in a relationship that will eventually help someone to draw closer to God. "Freely you have received, freely give." (Matthew 10:8)

Prayer for Today:

Dear God, open my eyes to see the people that are around me today. May I not be too self-absorbed to be used by You, and may I have wisdom and boldness to reach out. Amen.

Let the Young Folks Do It

Likewise, teach the older women to be reverent in the way they live, not to be slanderers or addicted to much wine, but to teach what is good. Then they can urge the younger women to love their husbands and children. Titus 2:3-4

Many young couples love backpacking but transition to drive-up tent camping when their children are born. Some purchase RVs when they tire of sleeping on the ground, then eventually give up camping altogether. In a similar way, young adults may begin their service to a church or ministry by volunteering for positions that require boatloads of energy (such as leading a group of middle school kids!) At some point they switch to other avenues of service, and many gradually pull away from responsibilities altogether. They feel that they have "paid their dues" and expect younger members of the group to pay their own. But is happiness truly found in pursuing activities that only benefit ourselves, such as hobbies, collections, or travel?

I've been fortunate to know many individuals and couples who have demonstrated that there is great joy and fulfillment in continuing to serve the Lord far past the age of retirement. Some who have returned from overseas work have sought out international students in our community in order to build relationships and show the love of Christ. Another couple spent more than half of each year traveling great distances by air to lead seminars designed to encourage pastors around the world. One woman volunteered to lead a women's ministry that included ladies from churches in three states, even though she knew that she would need help with the technology-related aspects of that position. Each of these individuals worked humbly, never calling attention to themselves, and their example impacted me greatly.

Determine before God that every day you are given breath you will use in service, love, and grace. If you have physical limitations, be a prayer warrior and look for ways to reach out and encourage others. No matter what your age, follow the advice that Titus gave to older women and be reverent, teach what is good, and take an active role to instruct and strengthen those who are younger than yourself. "Let everything that has breath praise the Lord." (Psalm 150:6)

Prayer for Today:

Dear God, thank you that today I have been given life and strength to serve You. Grant me willingness and initiative to step up and be used of You to show your love and grace to the world. May I be aware of the brevity of life, and may I not waste the days that You have given to me. Show me how to humbly be of service this day. Amen.

Heart Reflection

As water reflects the face, so one's life reflects the heart.
Proverbs 27:19

Lakeside camping brings many varied and wonderful views. On a particularly clear day, the surface of a lake may be calm enough to beautifully reflect the trees or mountains that surround it. You may even be able to get a mirrored view of your own face. Are you familiar with Narcissus, the character from Greek mythology who fell in love with his own reflection in a pool of water? Today, the term *narcissism* means an excessive fixation on oneself. Narcissists have difficulty empathizing with others and constantly want to be admired. Most of us are not pathologically centered upon ourselves, but it is still easy to default into constantly thinking about our own needs, to the point that we don't really see or care about the people around us .

Proverbs 27:19 reminds us that our life is a reflection of our heart. "As water reflects the face, so one's life reflects the heart. " This can manifest itself through our thoughts, words or actions. Jesus said, "For it is from within, out of a person's heart, that evil thoughts come," (Mark 7:21), and "the things that come out of a person's mouth come from the heart." (Matthew 15:18) Paul told the Roman believers of his deep thankfulness that they were now obeying Biblical teaching, thanks to a change in their hearts. "But thanks be to God that, though you used to be slaves to sin, you have come to obey from your heart the pattern of teaching that has now claimed your allegiance. (Romans 6:17) Most importantly, salvation is not a consequence of being born into a religious family or following rituals, but it is the outcome of true heart belief: "For it is with your heart that you believe and are justified." (Romans 10:10)

The next time you see a mirror-smooth lake, think about the state of your heart, as well as the life that flows from it. Have you truly called out to Christ in repentance and faith? If not, reach out for him today. "If you declare with your mouth, 'Jesus is Lord,' and believe in your heart that God raised him from the dead, you will be saved." (Romans 10:9) If you are already a Christ follower, is your heart still centered on yourself? Ask for the renewal and purification of your heart. "Since, then, you have been raised with Christ, set your hearts on things above, where Christ is, seated at the right hand of God." (Colossians 3:1) Are you discouraged? "Sing and make music from your heart to the Lord." (Ephesians 5:19) Do you tend to worry? "But I trust in your unfailing love; my heart rejoices in your salvation." (Psalm 13:5)

Prayer for Today:

Dear Jesus, I want my life to be the reflection of a pure heart. I believe that You paid the penalty for my sin, and I look to You for salvation. Please work in my life and change my heart so that I will think, speak, and act more like You. Amen.

The Light of the World

When Jesus spoke again to the people, he said, "I am the light of the world. Whoever follows me will never walk in darkness, but will have the light of life. John 8:12

Flashlights are a part of almost everyone's list of essential camping gear. They also remain on a potential birthday gift list for just about everyone I know: boys and girls of almost any age, as well as adults. Penlights, mag lights, headlamps, keychain lights, flashlights shaped like cartoon characters, emergency flashers - you get the idea. The more lights, the better!

Jesus said, "I am the light of the world. Whoever follows me will never walk in darkness, but will have the light of life." (John 8:12) What does that actually mean for his followers?

- Light illuminates the way so that we can stay on the right path. "*Your word is a lamp for my feet, a light on my path.*" (Psalm 119:105)
- Light represents purity. "This is the message we have heard from him and declare to you: God is light; in him there is no darkness at all." (1 John 1:5)
- Light is hated by evil ones. "It is shameful even to mention what the disobedient do in secret." (Ephesians 5:12)

71

- Light reveals all that is hidden. "He will bring to light what is hidden in darkness and will expose the motives of the heart." (1 Corinthians 4:5)
- Light represents the promised Messiah, Jesus. "The people walking in darkness have seen a great light; on those living in the land of deep darkness a light has dawned." (Isaiah 9:2)
- Light helps people to find the truth. "I have made you a light for the Gentiles, that you may bring salvation to the ends of the earth." (Acts 13:47)
- Light will be the hallmark of the risen Christ when He returns. "For the Son of Man in his day will be like the lightning, which flashes and lights up the sky from one end to the other." (Luke 17:24)

Prayer for Today:

Dear Jesus, You are the light of the world, and
You have the power to bring salvation to all.
You expose the hidden sins in my life, and You
will guide me into all truth if I will only look to
You. Transform my life into one of purity, and
may love for others embolden me to share your
light and grace with others. Amen.

Joy, Obedience, and Love

If you keep my commands, you will remain in my love, just as I have kept my Father's commands and remain in his love. I have told you this so that my joy may be in you and that your joy may be complete. My command is this: Love each other as I have loved you. John 15:10-12

Christians sometimes get the reputation of being dour stick in the muds, joy killers. This is unfortunate, because not only does this stereotype cause some to lack interest in pursuing a faith journey, but it also is not consistent with the truth of Scripture. Christians should be the most joyful people on Earth. We have received forgiveness, God's Holy Spirit lives within us to guide and encourage, and we have the sure hope of eternal life.

John 15:10 is interesting because Jesus specifically refers to his own joy, and he tells his disciples that this joy will be reflected in their lives if they will keep his commands. This will be a complete inner joy that is less dependent on circumstances than the temporary happiness of the surrounding culture. So even the Man of Sorrows must have conveyed a special joy to his followers. "At that time Jesus, full of joy through the Holy Spirit, said, 'I praise you, Father, Lord of heaven and earth, because you have hidden these things from the wise and learned, and revealed them to little children.'" (Luke 10: 21) Keeping Christ's commands is not intended to fill our lives with drudgery, but to unleash Christ's joy in our lives.

Just as obedience and joy are linked, so obedience and love also go hand in hand. Christ goes on to specify that one of his most essential commands is that we are to love each other, "as I have loved you." (John 15:12) "In fact, this is love for God: to keep his commands. And his commands are not burdensome." (1 John 5:3)

"We love because He first loved us." (1 John 4:19) How did Jesus demonstrate his love for us? By leaving the glories of heaven to enter our world, selflessly giving his life to pay the penalty for our sin. That's a highly committed kind of love!

Joy, obedience, and love: these should be the hallmarks of every believer. Each day, thank the Lord for his deep, sacrificial love for you. Ask him to help you walk in obedience to his commands and to love others. Reap the joyful benefit of walking in obedience and love: "The precepts of the Lord are right, giving joy to the heart." (Psalm 19:8)

Prayer for Today:

Dear God, I want to experience the joy that can come only from You. Help me to obey your commands today, especially the command to love others. It is encouraging to know that You demonstrated joy to your followers and that I can also experience deep, lasting joy. Amen.

74

Thru Hiker or Day Tripper?

If they had been thinking of the country they had left, they would have had opportunity to return. Instead, they were longing for a better country-a heavenly one. Therefore God is not ashamed to be called their God, for he has prepared a city for them. Hebrews 11:15-16

Those who plan to hike the entire Appalachian Trail commit to over 2,100 miles of walking, beginning at Springer Mountain, Georgia and ending at Mount Katahdin, Maine. Thru hikers generally begin their journey at the southern end of the trail in late March or early April in order to reach the northern terminus before snowy weather arrives. Day trippers enjoy hiking along portions of the trail but are lacking the time, physical endurance, or desire to complete the entire journey. At the end of their day hike, they plan to head back to the familiarity and comforts of home.

When Abraham was called by God to leave Ur, he had no expectation that he would ever return. He had no idea of his earthly destination, but God showed him day by day where to travel. His ultimate destination was heaven. Christians have been criticized for being "so heavenly minded that they are no earthly good". Certainly, we are to live in such a way that our lives are an encouragement to others, and our actions should make this world a better place. But we should always view

75

ourselves as visitors who are passing through to a heavenly home. The possessions, dwellings, and activities of this world should not be an end to themselves, and we should be willing to set aside the comfortable and familiar if we are called by God to step forward onto an unfamiliar pathway.

Hebrews Chapter 11 includes a roll call of faith. This list of individuals (such as Abel, Enoch, Noah, and Abraham) also includes descriptions of how each one's faith was put into action in specific ways. They all shared one thing in common: "All these people were still living by faith when they died. They did not receive the things promised; they only saw them and welcomed them from a distance, admitting that they were foreigners and strangers on the earth." They were committed to a faith journey through a world that was never their ultimate home.

Are you a day tripper in this world, focused on your earthly home? Or are you a thru hiker with your final destination always in mind?

Prayer for Today:

Dear God, may I never be so enamored with
this world that I forget that this life is a short
journey in the context of eternity. Help me not
to cling to familiar routines and places so much
that I'm unwilling to step out in service to You.
May my daily actions and attitudes honor you,
and may I remember that You are leading me to
a heavenly home.   Amen.

Kindling Strife

As charcoal to embers and as wood to fire, so is a quarrelsome person for kindling strife. Proverbs 26:21

In order to build a campfire that will start quickly and continue to burn, remember TKF: Tinder/Kindling/Fuel. Tinder is easily combustible material such as dry pine needles, wood shavings, or birch bark that will burn quickly for only a short while. You will sometimes observe people gently blowing on this primitive flame to provide it with oxygen as the fire spreads through the tinder. Before lighting your tinder, however, create an initial arrangement of kindling (small sticks, smaller than your thumb in diameter) that will keep the fire going for longer than the tinder would. As your primary structure begins to burn, you can add more kindling at its perimeter. When the kindling is burning steadily, you are finally ready to add fuel: larger sticks and logs that are the long-term energy source for your campfire.

Without kindling to bridge the gap between tinder and fuel, your fire building efforts will fail. The Bible reminds us, "Without wood a fire goes out; without gossip a quarrel dies down. As charcoal to embers and as wood to fire, so is a quarrelsome person for kindling strife." (Proverbs 26:20-21) It's interesting that gossip and quarrels are linked in these verses. Often, the same sorts of people that love to spread gossip are also argumentative individuals. The quarrelsome person is looking to "fan the flames" of heated discussion, often insisting on having the last word in an argument. Gossip is used as a weapon to malign the character of others and make themselves appear superior.

What is it like to dwell in a household with a quarrelsome person? Proverbs 21:9 says, "Better to live on a corner of the roof than share a house with a quarrelsome wife." (Proverbs 21:9). But it's not only wives who are warned not to be troublesome. "Don't have anything to do with foolish and stupid arguments, because you know they produce quarrels. And the Lord's servant must not be quarrelsome but must be kind to everyone, able to teach, not resentful. Opponents must be gently instructed, in the hope that God will grant them repentance leading them to a knowledge of the truth." (2 Timothy 2:23-25)

The next time you are tempted to share gossip, think of how that juicy morsel of information might spark division and conflict. When you are opposed and want to enter into an argument in person or on social media, pray that the individual who opposes you will find repentance and embrace the truth. Always seek to avoid quarrels that fuel strife.

Prayer for Today:

Dear God, put a guard over my heart and my
lips today. May I not engage in gossip or
useless arguments. I pray now for those who
oppose me. Grant them salvation and renewed
hearts, and may your truth prevail. Help me to
act with kindness this day. Amen.

Living Water

On the last and greatest day of the festival, Jesus stood and said in a loud voice, "Let anyone who is thirsty come to me and drink. Whoever believes in me, as Scripture has said, rivers of living water will flow from within them." John 7:37-38
Jesus answered, "Everyone who drinks this water will be thirsty again, but whoever drinks the water I give them will never thirst. Indeed, the water I give them will become in them a spring of water welling up to eternal life. John 4:13-14

Hiking the Grand Canyon from rim to rim is a grueling and potentially dangerous experience. Only certain trails have any potable water sources along the way, and the arid climate of Arizona allows your sweat to evaporate before you are truly aware that you are sweating. If you were forced to hike the entire trail and could only drink the water you hauled yourself, you would have to carry almost twenty pounds of water! So it is essential to double check with park rangers to be sure that the drinking water sources you are counting on along the trails are in good working order on the day of your hike.

Symptoms of dehydration are thirst, dark urine and less frequent urination, headache, and muscle cramps. If the dehydration is severe, you may also experience extremely dry skin, dizziness, rapid breathing, rapid heartbeat, confusion, or fainting. Always drink plenty of water long before these symptoms become noticeable.

79

When Jesus spoke to the Samaritan woman at a well near her town, He promised her that those who drink the water He provides will never thirst again. Christ was speaking of spiritual thirst. What would be some symptoms of spiritual dehydration?

- a nagging sense of spiritual emptiness
- an unfulfilled desire to connect with God
- the realization that although we may feel happiness when circumstances are good, we have no consistent inner joy

Christ specifically chose to travel through Samaria and to engage the Samaritan woman in conversation, even though the Jews normally did not associate with Samaritans. He revealed a supernatural knowledge of many details of her life story and offered her grace, mercy, and fulfillment. The woman responded in faith and immediately left her water jars, running back into the nearby town to joyfully share of her encounter with the Messiah. If you feel physically thirsty today, rehydrate. If you feel spiritually thirsty today, seek the Savior who loves you.

Prayer for Today:

Dear Jesus, thank you so much that You
lovingly went out of your way to meet with the
Samaritan woman. You know every detail of
my life, and You still love me. As I read your
Word, please reveal yourself to me, and help
me to respond to You in faith. Thank you that
You promise to quench the thirst of my soul.
Amen.

Prunes Under a Biscuit

I appeal to you, brothers and sisters, in the name of our Lord Jesus Christ, that all of you agree with one another in what you say and that there be no divisions among you, but that you be perfectly united in mind and thought. 1 Corinthians 1:10

I spent one summer working as a camp counselor in the foothills of the Appalachian Mountains. Most of the meals in the dining hall were pretty tasty, but at least one morning per week, small bowls of prunes were served along with breakfast. I detested prunes, but the counselors were expected to set a good example for the campers by eating all types of foods. My solution was to cut off a few tiny pieces, tuck them into some other foods, and gulp them down. The remaining prunes would be hidden under a carefully placed biscuit. It was worth foregoing the biscuit I loved in order to avoid the majority of the prunes.

Sometimes it takes more effort to put off an unpleasant task than to go ahead and work through it. For example, if I return from a camping trip and delay the job of cleaning a muddy tarp, the crumpled up plastic of the tarp can begin to stick together as it dries or even develop an offensive smell. Taking care of the task quickly would actually be less work in the end.

In the area of relationships, if we avoid the hard work of apologizing to someone, over time it becomes even more difficult to admit that we are wrong, and a relationship may be irrevocably severed. If church leaders don't privately confront those in our fellowship who participate in gossip or who stir up division, the problem often becomes public and causes a rift in the church body. The resulting lack of unity does not honor Christ, and the watching world will justifiably accuse the church of hypocrisy.

What difficult task can you accomplish today that will allow you to breathe a sigh of relief when finished? What steps can you take today to help maintain the unity of believers in your local fellowship?

Prayer for Today:

Dear Lord I know that I need self discipline in order to accomplish hard tasks. May the Holy Spirit prompt me to push forward with them. If reconciliation is needed, give me insight and a peaceful spirit. May all that I say and do today lead to purity of life and unity in the church. Amen.

Hanging On

We have this hope as an anchor for the soul, firm and secure.
Hebrews 6:19

The Crypt Lake Trail hike in Alberta, Canada has often been included in lists of Canada's best hikes because of its varied scenery and epic views. After reading many articles about this trail, my husband and I decided that it would be the perfect "midlife crisis" hike, and it certainly lived up to its billing. The journey begins by ferry, and travelers are given serious bear warnings as they cross Upper Waterton Lake. You are also warned that anyone who misses the ferry ride home will have to spend the night - not a pleasant prospect!

The 10.5 mile round-trip hike begins in an evergreen forest and continues past waterfalls and up a narrow, rocky trail across loose scree. Then the most interesting part begins. You must climb an 8-foot ladder, crawl through a natural tunnel, and then side step along a ledge while holding on for dear life to a steel cable that has been attached to the face of the rock. Finally, you arrive at gorgeous Crypt Lake, where you can pause briefly for lunch before heading back to the ferry dock.

While preparing for the trip, I read many contrasting reviews of the cable portion of the hike. Some people were unfazed, while others basically said, "If you slip, you die." So I insisted that we each purchase a climbing harness and carabiners so that we could hook on to the cable. We never used the equipment again after returning from that adventure, but it was worth every penny to avoid being paralyzed by fear! Attaching myself securely to the cable made all the difference.

The writer of Hebrews describes our spiritual hope as "an anchor for the soul, firm and secure." (Hebrews 6:19) An anchored soul will not be paralyzed by fear but can move forward into the future. A secured soul will always be held by the Lord, even if the person stumbles off the path for a time. A soul that is firmly attached to the hope of forgiveness and eternal life can even pass through the valley of the shadow of death without dread. Thank you, Lord, for hope that is as secure as the unchangeability of your character.

Prayer for Today:

Dear God, You never change, and You always
fulfill your promises. Thank you that hope in
You is more than wishful human thinking.
Hope is a firm anchor for my soul. So many in
this world need your hope. Please increase my
compassion and love for others, and grant me
boldness to share your truth.   Amen.

Flower Beds or Flower Fields?

Consider how the wild flowers grow. They do not labor or spin. Yet I tell you, not even Solomon in all his splendor was dressed like one of these. Luke 12:27

Formal gardens such as those found at an English manor have a structured, balanced sort of beauty. Perfectly measured pathways lead between colorful, manicured garden beds, and the effect can be visually stunning. Nature arboretums are often less formally presented, but they usually have a planned arrangement to highlight various local habitats. Both of these venues are interesting to visit, but many campers prefer the totally unstructured beauty found in springtime fields of grass, mountains aflame with the colors of autumn leaves, and even the solitary splendor of an individual wildflower. Closeup photography of a single flower or leaf will reveal complex details that testify to the creative power and wisdom of God. Jesus reminded his listeners that even elegant kingly robes are no match in beauty for the loveliness of the lilies of the field.

It's interesting to consider that there are millions of beautiful flowers in the world that will never be seen by humans. Perhaps God created them simply for his own enjoyment or as an outpouring of innovative energy. The flowers that we do have an opportunity to view have a positive effect on our emotions as they encourage inner joy and peace.

The lesson of the lilies of the field is part of a larger lesson by Jesus about worry. Christ said, "If that is how God clothes the grass of the field, which is here today, and tomorrow is thrown into the fire, how much more will he clothe you—you of little faith!" (Luke 12: 28). God provides clothing for the lilies in a lavish way, although the lilies can make no contribution to their attire. Because we can trust God to richly provide for our needs, we should concentrate on eternal pursuits. "And do not set your heart on what you will eat or drink; do not worry about it. For the pagan world runs after all such things, and your Father knows that you need them. But seek his kingdom, and these things will be given to you as well. " (Luke 12:29-31)

Prayer for Today:

Dear God, there is so much that I can learn from the wildflowers. Thank you for creating their beauty, and thank you for giving human beings a spirit that will respond to that beauty with joy. Help me not to worry about the basic needs of life that you have already promised to provide. May I focus on seeking your kingdom today. Amen.

Trapped

Don't have anything to do with foolish and stupid arguments, because you know they produce quarrels. And the Lord's servant must not be quarrelsome but must be kind to everyone, able to teach, not resentful. Opponents must be gently instructed, in the hope that God will grant them repentance leading them to a knowledge of the truth, and that they will come to their senses and escape from the trap of the devil, who has taken them captive to do his will. 2 Timothy 2:23-26

Ticks are annoying and dangerous creatures. They can carry many serious diseases such as Lyme disease and Rocky Mountain spotted fever. Their feeding process reads like a script from a horror movie: waiting on a path in grass or bushes with front legs hanging forward, climbing aboard a host, cutting the skin and inserting a feeding tube, and sucking the host's blood for several days (if they are not removed.) You definitely want to avoid this vampire flick and steer clear of being trapped in the grip of a tick!

In Paul's second letter to Timothy, he discusses problems that Timothy will face from people who oppose correct teaching. He describes those individuals as being in the trap of the devil, who has taken them captive to do his will. (2 Timothy 2:23-26)

-What are the characteristics of those who are trapped? They are quarrelsome, they make foolish arguments, and they are in captivity to evil. "Don't have anything to do with foolish and stupid arguments, because you know they produce quarrels." (2 Timothy 2:23)

-How can they escape the trap of evil? When a person hears correct teaching about Jesus and recognizes his own need for repentance, he can call out for forgiveness. "Opponents must be gently instructed, in the hope that God will grant them repentance leading them to a knowledge of the truth, and that they will come to their senses." (2 Timothy 2:25)

-How is a teacher of God's people supposed to act? "And the Lord's servant must not be quarrelsome but must be kind to everyone, able to teach, not resentful. " (2 Timothy 2:24)

-What other advice did Paul have for Timothy in his letter? Pass on correct teaching to reliable people who can then teach others. Be faithful, even in suffering. Cleanse yourself from sin so that you can be useful to God. Pursue righteousness, faith, love, and peace. (2 Timothy 2:2,3,20-22)

Prayer for Today:

Dear God, I don't want to be trapped in the grip of the devil. Forgive me of the sins that have taken hold of my life. I believe that Jesus gave his life to take the penalty for my sins, and I thank you for your forgiveness. Please help me not to be a quarrelsome person, and may I live in righteousness so that I can be useful in spreading your grace and truth to others. Amen.

A Resounding Gong

If I speak in the tongues of men or of angels, but do not have love, I am only a resounding gong or a clanging cymbal. 1 Corinthians 13:1

When we think of the famous love chapter in the Bible (1 Corinthians 13) we often rightly focus on the characteristics of love in action. "Love is patient, love is kind. It does not envy, it does not boast, it is not proud." (1 Corinthians 13:4) The verses continue with specific examples of the kind of love that God wants us to display. But the chapter begins with a harsh metaphor to depict a life that is devoid of love but filled with pious or pompous speech. "If I speak in the tongues of men or of angels, but do not have love, I am only a resounding gong or a clanging cymbal." (1 Corinthians 13:1).

Gongs and cymbals are certainly not peaceful instruments. A single resounding gong is often heard in cartoons as a singer is unceremoniously ushered off stage during a cringe-worthy performance. A clanging cymbal would quickly cause listeners to develop a headache. We obviously don't want to even consider that our speech might come across as that obnoxious to anyone.

So it's a good idea to honestly examine some ways in which our spoken messages might not reflect the love of Christ:

- pride-filled self congratulations
- telling a "joke" at someone else's expense
- interrupting others
- saying things that reveal we are not truly listening
- "holier than thou" criticism
- crass or crude language

"May these words of my mouth and this meditation of my heart be pleasing in your sight, LORD, my Rock and my Redeemer." (Psalm 19:14) "Set a guard over my mouth, LORD; keep watch over the door of my lips." (Psalm 141:3)

Prayer for Today:

Dear Lord, I do not want to be an irritating, noisy gong. Help me to carefully guard the words that come out of my mouth today. Increase the purity of my heart so that I will only speak gracious, loving words. Help me to listen more than I speak. Amen.

Forest Fireflies

*In him was life, and that life was the light of all mankind. The light
shines in the darkness, and the darkness has not overcome it.*
John 1:4-5

Many of us remember the childhood fun of catching
fireflies in our backyard or at a campground. These
luminescent creatures flash in specific patterns in order to
attract a mate. For 2-3 weeks of the year, some fireflies
synchronize their flashing, to such a degree that it appears the
entire forest is switching on and off. Congaree National Park
in South Carolina and Great Smoky Mountains National Park
in Tennessee host annual synchronous firefly viewing events.
These are so popular that a lottery has been implemented to
protect the wildlife habitat and allow visitors to more easily
witness the phenomenon. Scientists use soil moisture and
temperature to predict the best viewing dates.

Fireflies are not specifically mentioned in the Bible, but
their ability to produce their own light through a chemical
process is a testament to the awesome power and creativity of
God. In Job chapters 38 and 39, God reminds Job of the
miracles of creation and man's smallness in comparison to the
Almighty. "Where were you when I laid the earth's
foundation? Tell me, if you understand…Have you ever given

orders to the morning, or shown the dawn its place?...Have you journeyed to the springs of the sea or walked in the recesses of the deep?...What is the way to the place where the lightning is dispersed, or the place where the east winds are scattered over the earth?...Does the eagle soar at your command and build its nest on high?" (Job 38:4,12, 16, 24, and 39:27)

The light created by synchronous fireflies is dependent upon molecular oxygen and compounds called luciferins. It's interesting that another name for Satan is Lucifer, and the Latin word *lucifer* means "bearer of light". Paul reminded the Corinthian believers that "Satan himself masquerades as an angel of light." (2 Corinthians 11:14) But true light only comes from God. "This is the message we have heard from him and declare to you: God is light; in him there is no darkness at all." (1John 1:5) "When Jesus spoke again to the people, he said, 'I am the light of the world. Whoever follows me will never walk in darkness, but will have the light of life.'" (John 8:12) When we are born again into God's family and our sins are forgiven, God's light changes us from within. This is why Jesus also said to his disciples, "You are the light of the world." (Matthew 5:14)

Prayer for Today:

Dear God, the amazing creatures that You have made testify to your greatness. I cannot create my own light, but tiny fireflies can. I trust You to change me from the inside so that I can show the world the light which comes from You. Only your light can overcome this world's darkness. Amen.

Rejoice in Assurance

The seventy-two returned with joy and said, "Lord, even the demons submit to us in your name." He replied, "I saw Satan fall like lightning from heaven. I have given you authority to trample on snakes and scorpions and to overcome all the power of the enemy; nothing will harm you. However, do not rejoice that the spirits submit to you, but rejoice that your names are written in heaven." Luke 10:17-20

Jesus sent out seventy-two of his followers into nearby towns, ahead of his own arrival, to tell others about Him and even to perform miracles of healing in his name. Two by two they spread the word about Christ, and the response was often dramatic, as individuals were released from the power of demonic spirits. When the seventy-two returned to Jesus, overflowing with joy because of the powerful manifestation of God's power over the demons, Jesus made three interesting observations.

First, Jesus reminded his followers that He had been present at the moment in history when Satan was banished from heaven for his pride and disobedience. "I saw Satan fall like lightning from heaven." (Luke 10:18) What a statement! The next time someone wants to dismiss Jesus as merely a good human teacher, remind them that in this verse and in other Scriptures, Jesus is claiming to be eternal and equal with

93

God. If He is not equal with God and was telling the disciples a falsehood, then He cannot be good. But if the deity of Christ is true, then He deserves our full adoration and obedience.

Second, Christ assures them that his authority will grant them victory over all the power of the enemy. "I have given you authority to trample on snakes and scorpions and to overcome all the power of the enemy; nothing will harm you." (Luke 10:19) Christ's followers can rest in the powerful provision of God, and they should only use this special authority in a way that brings glory to him.

Finally, Jesus tells his followers that it is not the ability to wield dramatic power that should be the source of their greatest happiness. "However, do not rejoice that the spirits submit to you, but rejoice that your names are written in heaven." (Luke 10:20) The assurance that we are forever forgiven and have been granted the certain hope of eternal life is a promise that should bring deep, lasting joy.

Prayer for Today:

Dear Jesus, You are equal with God and
worthy of my worship and obedience. You
gave the disciples power to serve you, and You
will also enable me to faithfully live for You if
I follow your Word. You have the ability to
forgive my sins and grant eternal life, and I
thank and praise you for this great promise.
Amen.

Start 'Em Young

Start children off on the way they should go, and when they are old they will not turn from it. Proverbs 22:6

Do you remember your first camping trip? I don't - because I can never remember *not* camping. I am more than four years younger than my closest sibling, so I'm sure no one wanted to wait for me to grow out of toddlerhood before setting off on outdoor adventures with our family of six. The advantage to launching into camping at a very early age was that I quickly adjusted to falling asleep in a tent.

In the same way, even very young children can easily figure out that attending church is a natural, rewarding, and enjoyable experience if the family establishes a routine that includes worship as soon as possible after birth. Certainly, your child may go through a normal stage of "stranger anxiety" at about 12 months of age, and you will walk away from the church nursery with the sounds of your child's cries in your ears, but soon that stage will pass. Don't wait for the perfect time to start taking your sons and daughters to church or to other fellowship activities. Start them young and allow God's truth to permeate their lives.

If you have no children of your own, or your children have flown the nest, you can still participate in the spiritual formation of little ones. Even if you only serve as a last-resort alternate on a nursery volunteer list for the times when absolutely no one else is available, you will be fulfilling an important role that someone will truly appreciate. You can also look out for that shy, awkward middle school girl who is standing alone in the hallway and make an effort to learn her name and provide encouragement. If you don't feel comfortable interacting with children, perhaps you can provide technical or administrative support for a children's ministry. Everyone can pray for kids and workers individually. Pray that the hearts of the children you know will be tender, that they will respond to the love and grace of Jesus. Pray that those who have turned away from the training of their childhood will return to Jesus and find forgiveness and restoration.

Finally, remember that we can learn as much from children as they can from us. In the words of Christ, "Let the little children come to me, and do not hinder them, for the kingdom of God belongs to such as these. Truly I tell you, anyone who will not receive the kingdom of God like a little child will never enter it." (Luke 18:16-17)

Prayer for Today:

Dear Jesus, You cared for the children when You lived in this world, and they are just as important to You now. May I never ignore my responsibility to find some way to contribute to the spiritual growth of the children that You have placed around me. Show me specific ways that I can encourage them, and make me a positive example of what it means to follow You Amen

The Mummy's Curse

The understanding of this message will bring sheer terror. The bed is too short to stretch out on, the blanket too narrow to wrap around you.
Isaiah 28:19-20

Sleeping bags come in many sizes, materials, and shapes. Backpackers often choose a bag with a "mummy" shape in order to limit both weight and bulk, but some people just can't stand the restrictions that a mummy bag places on one's ability to move around in the night. You're basically forced to select a position and hope that you can fall asleep in that arrangement. Choosing a sleeping bag shaped like a rectangle or barrel will provide more freedom of movement, and even a loose-fitting blanket can provide a bit of warmth.

When the prophet Isaiah foretold the destruction of the leaders of Ephraim and Judah in Isaiah 28, he used the metaphor of an individual who tries to cover himself with a blanket that is too small: "The bed is too short to stretch out on, the blanket too narrow to wrap around you." (Isaiah 28:20) These leaders would soon experience God's judgement and would be unable to cover themselves to ensure their safety or to hide their wickedness. What exactly was the basis for this punishment? Isaiah records that the leaders of Ephraim and Judah were filled with pride and drunkenness. They scoffed at God and felt secure that judgement would never reach them.

How can we relate to this today? Most of us rarely drink too much or openly mock God, but what about pride? Here are some scriptural reminders about pride and how it can sneak into our lives:

- Pride occurs when our minds don't have room for God. "In his pride the wicked man does not seek him; in all his thoughts there is no room for God." (Psalm 10:4)
- Pride can be accompanied by strife and an unwillingness to listen to advice. "Where there is strife, there is pride, but wisdom is found in those who take advice." (Proverbs 13:10)
- Pride wants to exalt man over God. "The arrogance of man will be brought low and human pride humbled; the Lord alone will be exalted in that day." (Isaiah 2:17)
- Pride will never prevail. "And those who walk in pride he is able to humble." (Daniel 4:37)

The antidote to pride is to have a correct view of ourselves in relation to God, to humbly honor the Lord and others in all we do. "Do nothing out of selfish ambition or vain conceit. Rather, in humility value others above yourselves." (Philippians 2:3) A humble heart brings the blessing of God. "All of you, clothe yourselves with humility toward one another, because, 'God opposes the proud but shows favor to the humble.'" (1 Peter 5:5)

Prayer for Today:
Dear God, You are the awesome creator and sustainer of the universe. I humbly bring my prayer to You today. May I listen to wisdom and have a heart that is free of pride and conceit. Help me to treat others with love and respect, and may my life honor you this day. Amen.

Strangers or Angels?

*Do not forget to show hospitality to strangers, for by so doing some
people have shown hospitality to angels without knowing it*
Hebrews 13:2

Abraham, Lot, Gideon, and the parents of Samuel all
showed hospitality to strangers who turned out to be heavenly
messengers. In some of these cases, the visitor was not
initially revealed as an angel. God never promised that if we
show kindness to an angel in disguise that he would reveal the
secret to us right away, but showing hospitality is always a
noble act that can bring rewards in this life or the life to come.

Hospitality was highly prized in ancient Middle Eastern
culture and is still deeply valued today. It is considered normal
and honorable to go out of your way to serve those who come
into your home. Many overseas workers have spoken with
tears of instances in which impoverished families sacrificially
provided an elaborate meal for them, with the cost far
exceeding their limited means.

In the Bible, hospitality is listed as one of the prerequisites
for serving as a church elder (along with being a lover of what
is good, and being self-controlled, upright, holy, and
disciplined.) (Titus 1:8) It is also a character trait required for

99

widows who wish to receive financial support from the congregation. (1 Timothy 5:9-10) Peter reminded his readers to "offer hospitality to one another without grumbling. " (1 Peter 4:9)

How can we fulfill the command to be hospitable today? We are unlikely to have strangers appear at our doorstep who need a meal and lodging. But we can look for ways to serve others without expecting something in return. Hospitality can involve meals, clothing, time, helpful acts, and especially, love. "Do to others as you would have them do to you. If you love those who love you, what credit is that to you? Even sinners love those who love them. And if you do good to those who are good to you, what credit is that to you? Even sinners do that." (Luke 6:31-33)

"...serve one another humbly in love." (Galatians 5:13)

Prayer for Today:

Dear God, it can sometimes seem that I don't have many opportunities to be hospitable, but I am sure that situations already exist for showing hospitality that I have not even noticed. Please develop in me a willingness to serve without expecting anything in return. Give me creativity to find new ways to help others, and make me joyful and loving in every act of service. Amen.

Well Prepared

But in your hearts revere Christ as Lord. Always be prepared to give an answer to everyone who asks you to give the reason for the hope that you have. But do this with gentleness and respect. 1 Peter 3:15

The Boy Scout motto is "Be Prepared", but an equally wise motto for any camper might be "Be Prepared for Almost Anything". This is especially true in the area of clothing. Because it isn't practical to carry along suitcases full of apparel to fit every possible weather scenario, it is best to dress in layers. A T-shirt + long sleeved shirt + vest + fleece jacket will give you the warmth of an overcoat when worn together, but the individual components can be combined in countless ways to adapt to changes in temperature. Flexibility is key.

In the same way, we are instructed in the Scriptures to be prepared to share our faith at all times. "Always be prepared to give an answer to everyone who asks you to give the reason for the hope that you have." (1 Peter 3:15) Notice that we are to answer those who ask, not shout at those who aren't interested. But if our lives are marked by hope within, others will want to know the source of that hope. Peter also reminds us, "in your hearts revere Christ as Lord." (1 Peter 3:15) If Christ is truly our guide and king, his nature will become more and more apparent in us. Our attitudes and actions will grow more like those of Jesus, and this will be winsome to others.

Peter also reminds us to "do this with gentleness and respect." (1 Peter 3:15) Unfortunately, gentleness and respect are often not the hallmarks of Christians. When we have an opportunity to share the hope of forgiveness, transformation, and eternal life, it's crucial to take a moment to lift up a silent prayer, asking for a calm and loving spirit to control the tone and content of our words.

We don't have to spout out a memorized presentation, but we should learn some Scripture verses and think through some ideas before the opportunity to share ever arises. It can often be appropriate to share a bit of our own spiritual journey. And most people will be appreciative if we ask them if they would like for us to pray about anything for them.

Respectful speech, thoughtful mention of the Scriptures, genuine concern, and prayerfulness are all ways to share the hope that we have. Take some time to be prepared, pray for opportunities to arise, and then step through any open doors with a prayer in your heart and a willingness to be used by God.

Prayer for Today:

Dear God, You are my Lord and King today.
Bring my thoughts, words, and actions into line
with your Word. Thank you that You have
given me hope within. Grant me self-
discipline to prepare for the opportunities that
You will bring my way, and give me a gentle
and compassionate spirit.   Amen.

Enjoy the Moment Fully

Lord, our Lord, how majestic is your name in all the earth. You have set your glory in the heavens. Psalm 8:1

If a graph were to be made of the number of photographs taken on a typical camping trip over the course of my life, the graph would be shaped like a bell curve. During my teen years, I did not own a cell phone or a digital camera, so rolls of film had to be sent off for development. I didn't want to waste money to have scores of pictures printed, so I didn't take very many photos. When I acquired a cell phone with photo capabilities, I began to take more and more pictures on every trip, knowing that the "duds" could simply be deleted at a later time.

Recently I have found myself actually taking fewer photos than in the past. I want to live in the moment and enjoy soaking in views and vistas, rather than constantly covering my face with my phone. I want to focus on praising God for his beautiful creation, rather than on creating the perfect shot. When my trip is complete, my friends and relatives won't want to view a picture of every waterfall that I passed on each hike. The photographs can serve primarily as a record for myself, not as a way to establish social media bragging rights for the ultimate vacation.

If my children or grandchildren are participating in an event or celebrating a milestone, I can take a few pictures but remain committed to truly being there emotionally for them; a loving relative rather than a member of the paparazzi. I still have a long way to go in this area, but I plan to challenge myself to bask in the beauty of our world and in the joy of experiences as they occur without immediately reaching for a camera or phone. I want to become more faithful to follow the Lord's advice, "Be still, and know that I am God." (Psalm 46:10)

Prayer for Today:

Dear God, there is so much beauty to enjoy in your world and so many precious moments to be spent with those we love. May I focus on your world and your people, rather than being preoccupied with recording them. Amen.

Spur One Another On

Let us hold unswervingly to the hope we profess, for he who promised is faithful. And let us consider how we may spur one another on toward love and good deeds, not giving up meeting together, as some are in the habit of doing, but encouraging one another - and all the more as you see the Day approaching. Hebrews 10:23-25

I recently saw a bumper sticker that proclaimed, "Nature is my Church." Notice that it did not say, "Nature is my God". That would be considered idolatry. Romans 1:25 states, "They exchanged the truth about God for a lie, and worshiped and served created things rather than the Creator".

So can nature ever serve as a church? Nature can certainly point us to God. "The heavens declare the glory of God; the skies proclaim the work of his hands." (Psalm 19:1) The natural world can also reveal aspects of God's character. "For since the creation of the world God's invisible qualities-his eternal power and divine nature-have been clearly seen, being understood from what has been made, so that people are without excuse." (Romans 1:20) Nature can also bring serenity and joy to our souls. God will not condemn us for missing an occasional Sunday morning church service in order to rest in his magnificent creation. Yet nature (or online services, for that matter) can never truly be a good substitute for the fellowship, accountability, and opportunities to serve that are found within a local church body.

The early church was committed to meeting together. "They devoted themselves to the apostles' teaching and to fellowship, to the breaking of bread and to prayer...Every day they continued to meet together in the temple courts. They broke bread in their homes and ate together with glad and sincere hearts, praising God and enjoying the favor of all the people." (Acts 2:42, 46-47) But somewhere along the line, some had given up their regular times of assembly. In Hebrews 10:23-25, the author urges the Hebrew Christians to resume their meetings for a number of reasons that are still true today:

- meet in order to keep strong in the hope that we profess
- meet because Christ is faithful
- meet to encourage each other in love
- meet to spur one another to works of service
- meet because the day of Christ's return is approaching

On days when you are surrounded by nature, lift your heart in adoration and praise to the Lord. If you have been turned off by the hypocritical actions of some in the church, ask God for healing and guidance to find a new fellowship group. Seek out the company of those who will challenge and support you as you grow in your faith.

Prayer for Today:

Dear God, thank you that others can help me
walk closer to You. Help me to find a church
that correctly teaches God's word, and give me
a desire to serve You better along with others.
Amen.

Evergreen

But blessed is the one who trusts in the Lord, whose confidence is in him. They will be like a tree planted by the water that sends out its roots by the stream. It does not fear when heat comes; its leaves are always green. It has no worries in a year of drought and never fails to bear fruit. Jeremiah 17:7-8

Evergreen trees provide four seasons of consistent beauty, but did you know that there are more evergreen species than just conifers? Holly, live oak, magnolia, and some rainforest trees are also considered to be evergreens because they only replace their leaves or needles a few at a time throughout the year, so there is little change in the overall appearance of the tree. Yet even an evergreen plant could turn brown and wither if it is affected by disease or drought.

In the Bible, a green plant is often used as a metaphor for a spiritually healthy person. Stressful situations (heat) and times of physical or emotional need (drought) cannot succeed in drying up the plant or rendering it unable to bear fruit. Even in these difficult circumstances, fear or worry are not allowed to flourish. "It does not fear when heat comes; its leaves are always green. It has no worries in a year of drought and never fails to bear fruit." (Jeremiah 17:8).

What are the characteristics of this person whose faith is hardy and vigorous? First, the healthy believer has trust and confidence in the Lord. "But blessed is the one who trusts in the Lord, whose confidence is in him." (Jeremiah 17:7). Second , the person is rooted in Christ, drawing spiritual life from Him. "So then, just as you received Christ Jesus as Lord, continue to live your lives in him, rooted and built up in him. (Colossians 2:6-7) If the roots are not deep and strong, the water cannot nourish the plant, and the plant will die. "Those on the rocky ground are the ones who receive the word with joy when they hear it, but they have no root. They believe for a while, but in the time of testing they fall away." (Luke 8:13) Finally, the spiritually healthy individual continues to increase in faith and thankfulness, "rooted and built up in him, strengthened in the faith as you were taught, and overflowing with thankfulness." (Colossians 2:7)

Let us follow the advice of Jesus in this matter: "I am the vine, you are the branches. If you remain in me and I in you, you will bear much fruit; apart from me you can do nothing." (John 15:5) May our leaves be always green and our lives always fruitful.

Prayer for Today:

Dear Lord, thank you for your promises. I'm
so glad that fear and worry don't have to
control me, no matter the circumstances. I'm
thankful that my life can be fruitful if I remain
dependent upon You. Help me to rest
confidently in your promises this day and
always. Amen.

108

Zip it Up!

...you may be sure that your sin will find you out. Numbers 32:23

"Keep the tent zipped!!" My father's voice rang out heatedly after he discovered the tent zipper left open. It had been all too easy to pop into the tent to grab something I had forgotten, thinking that no one would be the wiser if I left the front screen unzipped just for a moment. Naturally, I had been found out. At the time, I probably thought that he was overreacting, but any mosquito or gnat that might have found its way into the tent would have been all too apparent later that evening as family members tried to fall asleep. My negligence and lack of attention to detail would have caused problems for all six of us.

In the same way, it's easy to think that small indiscretions, untruths, tidbits of gossip, or negative attitudes aren't really hurting anyone. The effects of our actions, words, and thoughts might not be apparent at first, but over time they can build up and begin to impact our own lives and the lives of those around us. How can these sins that we believe to have little importance cause so much difficulty?

- Even "hidden" disobedience to God's best plan for us is not hidden to God.

- We will know in our hearts that we have harbored poor attitudes or engaged in negative actions, and these will cause a weight of guilt.
- We may try to cover up our disobedience by inventing new lies.
- If our walk doesn't match our talk, those around us who do not believe in God will rightly label us as hypocrites.
- If we become comfortable with small indiscretions, it becomes easier to commit greater indiscretions.
- God's will is good, acceptable, and perfect. Stepping aside from God's road ultimately leads away from joy and blessing.

Jesus told his disciples, "Be on your guard against the yeast of the Pharisees, which is hypocrisy. There is nothing concealed that will not be disclosed, or hidden that will not be made known." (Luke 12:1-2) Yeast in its package just looks like harmless dust, but when the yeast is added to warm water, it soon causes the liquid to bubble up as a chemical change takes place. The "yeast" of the Pharisees, according to Jesus, was their hypocrisy. These religious leaders prided themselves in outward adherence to religious rules, but their sins were apparent to Jesus. Eventually, the hypocrisy of the Pharisees would become apparent to all.

Prayer for Today:

Dear Lord, your followers are often accused of hypocrisy, and at times the accusation is true. I don't want to be guilty of pretending to honor You while harboring "small" sins that will eventually lead to bigger issues in my life. I trust You to help me purify my heart attitudes, actions, and words today. Amen.

Soaring

Even youths grow tired and weary, and young men stumble and fall; but those who hope in the Lord will renew their strength. They will soar on wings like eagles; they will run and not grow weary, they will walk and not be faint. Isaiah 40:30-31

Bald eagles can fly at heights of over 11,000 feet, far above the altitude frequented by most birds but not too high to hone in on prey and swoop down at astounding speeds of up to 100 miles per hour. It is indeed a rich promise from God that "those who hope in the Lord will renew their strength. They will soar on wings like eagles." (Isaiah 40:31) How often our strength needs to be renewed! These verses never promise that our strength will be an unbroken flow, but it assures us that the Lord will recharge our energy, stability, and capability when we feel we have no more to muster. This passage is the conclusion of the fortieth chapter of the Book of Isaiah, a chapter that is overflowing with promises from God. Here are some of the highlights:

- The Messiah is coming. "A voice of one calling: 'In the wilderness prepare the way for the Lord; make straight in the desert a highway for our God'" (Isaiah 40:3)
- God's Word never fails. "The grass withers and the flowers fall, but the word of our God endures forever." (Isaiah 40:8)

- The Lord deals with us tenderly. "He tends his flock like a shepherd; He gathers the lambs in his arms and carries them close to his heart." (Isaiah 40:11)
- God is awesome in creativity and power. "Lift up your eyes and look to the heavens: Who created all these? He who brings out the starry host one by one and calls forth each of them by name. Because of his great power and mighty strength, not one of them is missing." (Isaiah 40:26)

The faithful Creator who holds all power, the one who loved us so much that He sent his Son to pay the penalty for our sins, the one who keeps his promises and deals with us in tenderness - this is the one who has pledged to renew your strength.

Prayer for Today:

Dear God, I need your strength today. Thank you for the example of the eagle, who soars with the strength that You give. I trust You because You are faithful and true. Amen.

Fish out of Water

I am against you, Pharaoh king of Egypt, you great monster lying among your streams. You say, "The Nile belongs to me; I made it for myself." But I will put hooks in your jaws and make the fish of your streams stick to your scales... I will leave you in the desert, you and all the fish of your streams...Then all who live in Egypt will know that I am the Lord. Ezekiel 29:3-6

We enjoy camping in Corps of Engineers Campgrounds because they are almost always situated on lakes, they have campsites that are not too close together, and the price is extremely inexpensive (especially if you have a National Parks Pass.) These campgrounds are often filled with water sports enthusiasts, so it's not uncommon to see kayaks and life jackets sitting nexts to tents, as well as boats trailers heading to and from the boat launch area.

Have you ever tried to get a boat out of the water and onto a trailer? The boat ceases its graceful gliding and becomes an awkward, heavy vessel that is about as difficult to maneuver as a beached whale. Once the bow of the craft has been guided onto the trailer, the owner must use a winch to pull up the remainder of the boat. Truly a fish out of water!

Of course, a fish cannot survive once it has left its aquatic home, so removing a fish from water condemns it to imminent death. In the Book of Ezekiel, the prophet pronounces a similar judgement on Pharaoh and the people of Egypt. During the next forty years, Egypt would become desolate and ruined, and even though the Egyptians would eventually be returned to the land of their ancestry, Egypt would never completely regain its prior strength and power. What was the reason for this severe judgement by God? The prophet denounces Pharaoh because he does not acknowledge God as creator and ruler. "You say, 'The Nile belongs to me; I made it for myself.'" (Ezekiel 29:3)

The prophet Isaiah brings similar words of judgement to Israel, because Israel has sinned and has displayed a lack of trust in the faithfulness and omnipotence of God. "Because of your sins you were sold; because of your transgressions your mother was sent away...Was my arm too short to deliver you? Do I lack the strength to rescue you? By a mere rebuke I dry up the sea, I turn rivers into a desert; their fish rot for lack of water and die of thirst." (Isaiah 50:1-2)

Prayer for Today:

Dear God, You created everything, and You order the events of history. You have always sustained and helped those who humbly trust in You. Thank you that your Word contains so many examples of your faithful provision and your mighty power. Amen.

Bushwhacking

Enter through the narrow gate. For wide is the gate and broad is the road that leads to destruction, and many enter through it. But small is the gate and narrow the road that leads to life, and only a few find it.
Matthew 7:13-14

Bushwhacking - does it really save time and effort? Going off-trail as a short cut is tempting. It can also be a fun challenge if you are experienced with a compass and terrain map. But you will need to take serious precautions to ensure your safety. Long pants and sleeves are a must (they don't call it bushwhacking for nothing!) Be aware of terrain obstacles and possible steep elevation changes. Avoid being out after dark in an unfamiliar area without proper gear. Basically, unless you are well prepared and enjoy the challenge, don't do it! Tried and true trails will generally be faster and safer, and hiking an established narrow path will likely be more successful than launching out across an untested course.

The term *narrow* generally has a negative view in our culture. A narrow-minded person is seen as someone with a very limited way of seeing the world. *Bigoted, intolerant*, and *old-fashioned* are terms often used as synonyms for *narrow*. But Jesus specifically referred to a narrow gate and a narrow road when speaking of the way to eternal life. "Enter through the narrow gate. For wide is the gate and broad is the road that leads to destruction, and many enter through it." (Matthew 7:13) Jesus also said, "I am the way and the truth and the life. No one comes to the Father except through me." (John 14:6)

Imagine that you have a very serious illness. Your doctor is experienced and well trained, and she recommends a very specific course of action, the only path that has proven to be effective . Little benefit would come from arguing, "I think your advice is too narrow. There are so many possible roads to getting better. I'll try other treatments." She cares about you and has shown you the way to health, but you refuse to listen. Jesus once lamented, "Jerusalem, Jerusalem, you who kill the prophets and stone those sent to you, how often I have longed to gather your children together, as a hen gathers her chicks under her wings, and you were not willing. " (Matthew 23:37)

If you are unsure whether Jesus told the truth about the narrow path to heaven, sincerely seek God's will and ask for insight. Christ promised, "Anyone who chooses to do the will of God will find out whether my teaching comes from God or whether I speak on my own." (John 7:17) He also gave this assurance: "If you hold to my teaching, you are really my disciples. Then you will know the truth, and the truth will set you free." (John 8:31-32)

Prayer for Today:
Dear Jesus, when You tell us to enter by the
narrow gate, You are not being uncaring.
Rather, You love us enough to tell us exactly
how to find the correct path to peace with God.
You demonstrated your love when You died for
our sins. Help me to reach out in faith for
restoration and forgiveness. Amen.

Heaps of Stones

So Jacob took a stone and set it up as a pillar. He said to his relatives, "Gather some stones." So they took stones and piled them in a heap, and they ate there by the heap…Laban also said to Jacob, "Here is this heap, and here is this pillar I have set up between you and me. This heap is a witness, and this pillar is a witness, that I will not go past this heap to your side to harm you and that you will not go past this heap and pillar to my side to harm me. Genesis 31: 45-46, 51-52

Have you ever been hiking along and have unexpectedly come upon a stack of stones artistically balanced upon each other? These piles of stones, called cairns, are often used as trail markers, especially on trails that do not have tree blazes. On rocky "bald" areas, a cairn may be the only thing that keeps you from missing an important turn or stepping off a hidden ledge.

Cairns have been used by humans for a variety of purposes throughout history, such as survey markers, burial monuments, and religious ceremonial structures. Laban and Jacob used a cairn as a boundary marker in Genesis 31. The Book of Proverbs includes more than one admonition not to move an ancient boundary stone. (Proverbs 22:28 and 23:10) Joshua was instructed by God to erect a cairn at Gilgal from twelve stones that had been carried up from the middle of the Jordan River during the miraculous crossing of the river on dry land. (Joshua 4) After a victory in battle over the Philistines, Samuel set up a stone and said, "Thus far the Lord has helped us." (1 Samuel 7:12)

In a similar way, it can be helpful to memorialize important events in our spiritual lives as a way of keeping them fresh in our mind. If we have made a faith commitment, it's a good idea to write down the date and the promise that we made at that time in our Bible or journal. If God has shown his faithfulness in a specific way, we can share about the circumstances in a conversation or a letter that will encourage others and fortify us to step out in faith in the future. It can also be helpful to write down and post in your home some words from a particular song or some verses from the Scriptures that bring to mind the love, power, and steadfastness of God.

Prayer for Today:

Dear God, I think now of commitments that I
have made in the past to follow and obey You.
I renew them in my mind and heart even now.
I think of particular ways that You have
demonstrated your faithfulness, and I trust You
to lead me in the future. Please grant me
opportunities to tell others of what You have
done for me, and make me brave and
determined to follow through in declaring your
greatness and your lovingkindness. Amen.

Joy in the Morning

Satisfy us in the morning with your unfailing love, that we may sing for joy and be glad all our days. Psalm 90:14

Are you satisfied? That depends on the context. If I've just stuffed myself with burgers cooked on the grill, my appetite is satisfied. (At least until someone brings out the dessert!) If I've discovered a wonderful new hiking spot, my sense of adventure is satisfied. (At least until the novelty of my experience wears off.) It's all too easy to be dissatisfied with various parts of our lives: our appearance, our health, our wealth, our love life, or even our opportunities for travel and relaxation. The Bible says that "godliness with contentment is great gain" (1 Timothy 6:6), and it's certainly true that lasting joy can never be found if we are not content.

One key to joy and gladness is to rest in the unfailing love of God. "Satisfy us in the morning with your unfailing love, that we may sing for joy and be glad all our days." (Psalm 90:14) This may seem like a vague path to joy, but the concept can be made more specific. Perhaps I feel dissatisfied because my friend owns a beach cabin, while I make do with inexpensive day trips to the shore. I can remind myself that God's love for me is equal to God's love for my friend, and remember that He has never failed to fulfill his promises to me.

Perhaps my mornings are often filled with stress and worry. I can begin each morning with prayers of thanksgiving or post encouraging Bible verses on my mirror to put myself in the right frame of mind for the day. Perhaps the news on TV creates a longing in my heart for the relative security of my childhood. I can pray for those who live in difficult circumstances and sing joyful songs that help me recollect truths about the nearness of God in times of trouble.

Satisfaction and joy can never be consistent in our lives if they are based upon material possessions, upcoming job opportunities, or the approval of others. Isaiah 55:1-3 is a tender reminder of this: "Come, all you thirsty, come to the waters; and you who have no money, come, buy and eat! Come, buy wine and milk without money and without cost. Why spend money on what is not bread, and your labor on what does not satisfy? Listen, listen to me, and eat what is good, and you will delight in the richest of fare. Give ear and come to me; listen, that you may live. I will make an everlasting covenant with you, my faithful love promised to David." Jesus echoed these truths when he told the Samaritan woman at the well, "whoever drinks the water I give them will never thirst. Indeed, the water I give them will become in them a spring of water welling up to eternal life." (John 4:14).

Prayer for Today:

Dear God, I know that I need contentment in
order to have fullness of joy. Thank you for all
You have given me, and thank you for your
unfailing love. Please keep me joyful,
thankful, and satisfied this day. Amen.

About the Author

Nancy Bell Kimsey is a lifelong outdoor enthusiast whose hiking and camping experiences have ranged from backpacking and family tent camping to adventuring in a fiberglass travel trailer.   She moved to North Carolina to attend Wake Forest University and remained in the Tar Heel State throughout her career as an educator. She is a contributing writer for a number of camping publications and the author of *Grace on a Rambling Road: Devotions for RV Travelers.*

About the Author

Printed in the USA
CPSIA information can be obtained
at www.ICGtesting.com
CBHW020738090824
12943CB00031B/159